" Leaning on the everlasting arms "

Love, Patty

Let My Soul Look Up

Timeless Inspiration for a 21st Century World!

Patty Ellis

WESTBOW
PRESS®
A DIVISION OF THOMAS NELSON
& ZONDERVAN

WestBow Press books may be ordered through booksellers or by contacting:

WestBow Press
A Division of Thomas Nelson & Zondervan
1663 Liberty Drive
Bloomington, IN 47403
www.westbowpress.com
1 (866) 928-1240

ISBN: 978-1-9736-5968-6 (sc)
ISBN: 978-1-9736-5967-9 (hc)
ISBN: 978-1-9736-5969-3 (e)

Library of Congress Control Number: 2019904387

Print information available on the last page.

WestBow Press rev. date: 05/17/2019

For in Him we live and move and have our being;
as certain of your own poets have said.
—Acts 17:28

Contents

Preface

Words, Words, Words

> Not a burden we bear,
> Not a sorrow we share,
> But our toil He doth richly repay;
> Not a grief or a loss,
> Not a frown or a cross,
> But is blessed if we trust and obey.

I have no idea when it began to dawn on me that something, somewhere in the deepest shadows of my sadness, was stirring. Despite the suffocating despair that had wrapped its foul haze around my soul for so long, I cautiously began to sense a faint, almost mystical awareness—barely discernible, but it was there! I felt it! And it came from the most surprising source.

Having spent practically my entire life playing the piano in churches, my emotional focus as well as my physical energy had always been concentrated on the music score that lay before me. I knew just about every hymn in print and had played them countless times. I had recorded an album of my own hymn arrangements and performed hundreds of solo piano concerts. Music was my deal. The lyrics to all those hymns? Well, they were just a mishmash of lovely background noise—or so I thought.

> Abide with me, fast falls the eventide;
> The darkness deepens, Lord, with me abide.
> When other helpers fail, and comforts flee,
> Help of the helpless, O, abide with me.

Night and day, these *words* began coming to me. They came, they went—different lines of words I had been hearing all my life but had never really *heard*. As if from another reality, each new set brought its own unique significance to my parched spirit, and as one would fade away, another set would emerge. They were unsolicited but never unwanted. It seemed I was hearing these amazing, inspiring, beseeching words for the first time in my life.

I began to pay very close attention to the wise old words, every new remembrance pressing its precious imprint onto my gloomy heart. As more and more of these poignant lines came to mind, I felt compelled to write them down. I began a log of the songs each new day would bring, and to my utter amazement, they were instantly and warmly familiar to me—like an old, trusted friend I hadn't heard from in years. I searched the scriptures seeking passages which I could envision these authors reading and using as inspiration for the amazing words they would compose. (The added quote you will find for each hymn is another reminder of the enduring wisdom they embrace.)

At times, the words were magnificent and immense:

> Immortal, invisible, God only wise;
> In light inaccessible hid from our eyes.
> Most blessed, most glorious, the Ancient of Days,
> Almighty, victorious, Thy great Name we praise!

Sometimes, they were somber pleadings for mercy:

> Savior, Savior,
> Hear my humble cry;
> While on others Thou art calling,
> Do not pass me by.

They could be the simplest of lyrics:

> Jesus loves me, this I know,
> For the Bible tells me so.
> Little ones to Him belong,
> They are weak, but He is strong.

Or they could set my soul alive in rhythmic joy:

> By and by, when the morning comes,
> When the saints of God are gathered home,
> We will tell the story how we've overcome,
> For we'll understand it better by and by.

I searched through closets and cabinets for every hymnal I owned and, for the first time, pored over the *words* found on those worn pages. I combed through and researched every fragment of information I could find about these new, but familiarly old, revelations—their histories, their authors, and, most importantly, their place in the story of Christendom. It soon became obvious each had originated as beautiful poetry, and while some had been quickly noticed and set to music, most were not.

Most of this poetry had existed for decades, even centuries, before finally being discovered, translated if need be, and ultimately paired with a melody. In due course, the new "hymn" would appear in the most recently published hymnbook and would be introduced to crowds attending revival meetings and church gatherings. Slowly, the new hymn's popularity would spread, and it would become an integral part of mainstream worship services.

I began to appreciate that the men and women who composed these lines, like the scribes who wrote the incomparable prose and poetry that became our Holy Bible, had been divinely led. Just as God inspired kings, poets, fishermen, and prophets throughout the ages to set down His Holy Word, He also touched the hearts and souls of countless men and women to pen poetry so meaningful that it would become cherished and celebrated for centuries to come. Stirred by personal tragedies, losses, longings, and circumstances, these writers were led to put words to paper that would, in God's beautiful timing, weave their message into the very fabric of Christian culture and, most particularly, into the souls of believers throughout the world.

What was *not* to be found among these striking nuggets of wisdom was any mention of self-pity, self-righteousness, or self-indulgence. These poems had been written by people experiencing the depths of human anguish, hardship, and loss—but you will find no excuse-making here. Small wonder these were the songs our forebearers rallied around as they shaped the very foundations of our great nation. These were the words they intoned as they marched through the horrendous atrocities of the Civil War, World War I, the Great Depression, and World War II.

These were the hymns occupying our ancestors' thoughts and prayers as they plowed their fields, scrubbed at their washboards, fought disease and deprivation, and nursed family members who would never recover from illnesses we hardly take notice of today. These were the words that echoed through their souls as they experienced the greatest losses life can bring—except they had no government subsidies or insurance programs to fall back on. When famine, plague, devastation and death shattered their very existence, these glorious words fortified their endurance and emboldened their courage. Holding hymnbooks in weary but trusting hands, our forebearers sang these very songs, courageously facing trials and tribulations we cannot begin to imagine in today's world.

In all my searching, I never came across a poem in which the author offered assurances that we are God's spectacular little darlings who deserve to be lavished with every desire. I did not find one hymn that promised a road of ease, a life of luxury, or a trouble-free existence here on this earth. What each writer does assure, however, is that there is marvelous, unfailing grace and peace offered to each and every mortal soul – grace to sustain and comfort us no matter our circumstances – and peace surpassing all human understanding.

The writers concluded again and again that whatever burden we bear, whatever sorrow we carry, through prayer and faith, we *can* find comfort and we *can* endure. Trials are inevitable, disappointments are unavoidable, and distress and misfortune are certain—but life's tribulations need not define the end of our story. They can, quite miraculously, be just the beginning.

Reading and praying the words of these glorious old hymns took me on a journey I never saw coming—a journey that transformed my life. These sacred lines, like seeds destined to produce their bounty in an unknown future, restored my soul, reawakened my faith, and left me with a renewed measure of hope, joy and peace long missing from my life. Whether you, like me, will find these words among your earliest memories or you are reading them for the very first time, my prayer is that they will accomplish God's work in your heart and life just as they have done in mine.

This book is lovingly dedicated to my mother,
Florene Williamson,
whose steadfast resolve saw to it that her three daughters
never missed a church service or a piano lesson.
Her faithfulness still whispers throughout my days.

I Need Thee Every Hour

I need Thee every hour,
Stay Thou nearby.
Temptations lose their power
When Thou art nigh.

Hiding in Thee

In the tempests of life,
On it's wide, heaving sea,
Thou blessed Rock of Ages,
I'm hiding in Thee.

In Heavenly Love Abiding

In heavenly love abiding,
No change my heart shall fear;
And safe is such confiding,
For nothing changes here.

The storms may roar around me,
My heart may low be laid;
But God is round about me,
And can I be dismayed?

Wherever He may guide me,
No want shall turn me back;
My Shepherd is beside me
And nothing can I lack.

His wisdom ever waketh,
His sight is never dim;
He knows the way He taketh,
And I will walk with Him.

Green pastures are before me,
Which yet I have not seen.
Bright skies will soon be over me,
Where the dark clouds have been.

My hope I cannot measure,
My path to life is free.
My Savior has my treasure,
And He will walk with me.

Anna Letitia Waring (1820–1910)

God's Word

Give thanks to the God of heaven!
For His steadfast love endures forever.
—Psalm 136:26

"If you abide in Me,
and My words abide in you,
you will ask what you desire,
and it shall be done unto you."
—John 15:7

But you, O Lord, are a God
full of compassion, and gracious;
longsuffering and abundant in mercy and truth.
—Psalm 86:15

Reflection

Trust in yourself and you are doomed to
disappointment.
But trust in God and you are never to be
confounded in this time or in eternity.
—Dwight L. Moody (1837–1899)

He Leadeth Me! O Blessed Thought

He leadeth me,
O, blessed thought.
O, words with heavenly comfort fraught.
Whatever I do, wherever I be,
It is God's hand that leadeth me.

Sometimes 'mid scenes of deepest gloom,
Sometimes where Eden's bowers bloom,
By waters still,
Over troubled seas,
Still 'tis His hand that leadeth me.

And when my task on earth is done,
When by Thy grace the victory's won.
Even death's cold wave
I will not flee,
Since God through Jordan leadeth me.

He leadeth me, by His own hand,
He leadeth me.
His faithful follower I would be,
For by His hand,
He leadeth me.

Joseph H. Gilmore (1834–1918)

God's Word

You in Your mercy have led forth the people
whom You have redeemed;
You have guided them in Your strength
to Your holy habitation.
—Exodus 15:13

The Lord is my Shepherd;
I shall not want.
He makes me to lie down in green pastures;
He leads me beside still waters.
He restores my soul;
He leads me in the paths of righteousness
for His name's sake.
Yea, though I walk through the valley of the shadow of death,
I will fear no evil;
for You are with me.
—Psalm 23:1–4

Your ears shall hear a word behind you, saying,
"This is the way, walk in it."
—Isaiah 30:21

Reflection

I know not the way God leads me,
but well do I know my guide.
—Martin Luther (1483–1546)

I Am Resolved

I am resolved no longer to linger,
Charmed by the world's delights;
Things that are higher,
Things that are nobler,
These have allured my sight.

I am resolved to go to the Savior,
Leaving my sin and strife;
He is the true One,
He is the just One,
He hath the words of life.

I am resolved to follow the Savior,
Faithful and true each day;
Heed what He sayeth,
Do what He willeth,
He is the living Way.

I am resolved to enter the kingdom,
Leaving the paths of sin;
Friends may oppose me,
Foes may beset me,
Still will I enter in.

I will hasten to Him,
Hasten so glad and free.
Jesus, greatest, highest,
I will come to Thee.

Palmer Hartsough (1844–1932)

God's Word

My child, do not forget My law,
but let your heart keep my commands;
for length of days and long life
and peace they will add to you.
—Proverbs 3:1–2

And the Lord, He is the One who goes before you.
He will be with you,
He will not leave you nor forsake you;
do not fear nor be dismayed.
—Deuteronomy 31:8

"And if it seems evil to you to serve the Lord,
choose for yourselves this day whom you will serve,
whether the gods which your fathers served
that were on the other side of the River,
or the gods of the Amorites, in whose land you dwell.
But as for me and my house,
we shall serve the Lord."
—Joshua 24:15

Reflection

If all of this world falls from the truth,
I stand!
—Saint Athanasius (293–373)

Hiding in Thee

O safe to the Rock that is higher than I,
My soul, in its conflicts and sorrows would fly.
So sinful, so weary, Thine would I be,
Thou blessed "Rock of Ages,"
I'm hiding in Thee.

In the calm of the noontide, in sorrow's lone hour,
In times when temptation casts over me it's power;
In the tempests of life,
On it's wide, heaving sea,
Thou blessed "Rock of Ages,"
I'm hiding in Thee.

How often in the conflict, when pressed by the foe,
I have fled to my refuge and breathed out my woe;
How often, when trials like sea billows roll,
Have I hidden in Thee,
O, Thou Rock of my soul.

Hiding in Thee,
Thou blessed "Rock of Ages,"
I'm hiding in Thee.

William O. Cushing (1823–1902)

God's Word

You are my hiding place;
You shall preserve me from trouble;
You shall surround me with songs of deliverance.
—Psalm 32:7

And he said,
"The Lord is my rock, my fortress and my deliverer;
the God of my strength, in whom I will trust;
my shield and the horn of my salvation.
My stronghold and my refuge;
my Savior, You save me from violence."
—2 Samuel 22:2–3

Do not fear, nor be afraid;
Have I not told you from that time,
and declared it?
—Isaiah 44:8

Reflection

Have courage then:
ask of God, not deliverance from your pains,
but strength to bear resolutely, all that He should please.
—Brother Lawrence (1614–1691)

Be Still, My Soul

Be still, my soul; the Lord is on thy side.
Bear patiently the cross of grief or pain.
Leave to thy God to order and provide;
In every change, He faithful will remain.
Be still, my soul; thy best thy heavenly Friend,
Through thorny ways, leads to a joyful end.

Be still, my soul; thy God doth undertake
To guide the future, as He has the past.
Thy hope, thy confidence let nothing shake;
All now mysterious shall be bright at last.
Be still, my soul; the waves and winds still know
His voice who ruled them while He dwelt below.

Be still, my soul; when dearest friends depart;
And all is darkened in the vale of tears.
Then shall thou better know His love, His heart,
Who comes to soothe thy sorrow and thy fears.
Be still, my soul; thy Jesus can repay
From His own fullness all He takes away.

Be still, my soul; the hour is hastening on
When we shall be forever with the Lord.
When disappointment, grief and fear are gone,
Sorrow forgot, love's purest joys restored.
Be still, my soul; when change and tears are past,
All safe and blessed we shall meet at last.

Be still, my soul; begin the song of praise
On earth, be leaving to thy Lord on high;
Acknowledge Him in all thy words and ways,
So shall He view thee with a well pleased eye.
Be still, my soul; the sun of life divine
Through passing clouds shall but more brightly shine.

Katherina von Schlegel (1697–1768)
Translated from German to English by Jane L. Borthwick (1813–1897)

God's Word

Be still and know that I am God.
—Psalm 46:10

A time to tear
and a time to mend,
a time to keep silent
and a time to speak.
—Ecclesiastes 3:7

The Lord will fight for you,
and you shall hold your peace.
—Exodus 14:14

Rest in the Lord, and wait patiently for Him;
do not fret because of him who prospers in his way,
because of the man who brings wicked schemes to pass.
—Psalm 37:7

Reflection

True silence is the rest of the mind.
It is to the spirit what sleep is to the body—
nourishment and refreshment.
—Sir William Penn (1621–1670)

All the Way My Savior Leads Me

All the way my Savior leads me,
What have I to ask beside?
Can I doubt His tender mercy,
Who through life has been my Guide?
Heavenly peace, divinest comfort,
Here by faith in Him to dwell,
For I know, whatever befall me,
Jesus doeth all things well.

All the way my Savior leads me,
Cheers each winding path I tread.
Gives me grace for every trial,
Feeds me with the living Bread.
Though my weary steps may falter
And my soul athirst may be,
Gushing from the rock before me,
A spring of joy I see.

All the way my Savior leads me,
Oh, the fullness of His love!
Perfect rest to me is promised
In my Father's house above.
When my spirit, clothed immortal,
Wings its flight to realms of day,
This my song through endless ages,
Jesus led me all the way.

Fanny Jane Crosby (1820–1915)

God's Word

And the Lord went before them by day
in a pillar of cloud to lead the way,
and by night in a pillar of fire to give them light,
so as to go by day and night.
He did not take away the pillar of cloud by day
or the pillar of fire by night from the people.
—Exodus 13:21–22

Search me, O God, and know my heart;
try me and know my anxieties;
and see if there is any wicked way in me,
and lead me in the way everlasting.
—Psalm 139:23–24

I am the Lord, your God,
who teaches you to profit,
who leads you in the way you should go.
—Isaiah 48:17

Reflection

Faith sees the invisible,
believes the unbelievable,
and receives the impossible.
—Corrie ten Boom (1892–1983)

I Need Thee Every Hour

I need Thee every hour,
Most gracious Lord;
No tender voice like Thine
Can peace afford.

I need Thee every hour,
Stay Thou nearby;
Temptations lose their power
When Thou art nigh.

I need Thee every hour,
In joy or pain;
Come quickly and abide,
Or life is in vain.

I need thee every hour,
Teach me Thy will;
And Thy rich promises
In me fulfill.

I need Thee every hour,
Most Holy One;
O make me Thine indeed,
Thou blessed Son.

I need Thee, yes, I need Thee;
Every hour I need Thee.
O bless me now, my Savior,
I come to Thee.

Annie S. Hawks (1836–1918)

God's Word

So that we may boldly say:
"The Lord is my helper;
I will not fear.
What can man do to me?"
—Hebrews 13:6

And He said unto me,
"My grace is sufficient for you,
for My strength is made perfect in weakness."
—2 Corinthians 12:9

Let us therefore come boldly to the throne of grace,
that we may obtain mercy
and find grace to help in time of need.
—Hebrews 4:16

Reflection

Let us keep close to Christ.
And cling to Him.
And hang on Him.
So that no power can remove us.
—Martin Luther (1483–1546)

My Shepherd Will Supply My Need

My Shepherd will supply my need,
Jehovah is His name.
In pastures fresh He makes me feed,
Beside the living stream.
He brings my wandering spirit back
When I forsake His ways,
And leads me, for His mercy's sake,
In paths of truth and grace.

When I walk through the shades of death,
Thy presence is my stay.
One word of Thy supporting breath
Drives all my fears away.
Thy hand, in sight of all my foes,
Doth still my table spread;
My cup with blessings overflows,
Thine oil anoints my head.

The sure provisions of my God
Attend me all my days;
O may Thy house be my abode,
And all my work be praise.
There would I find a settled rest,
While others go and come;
No more a stranger, not a guest,
But like a child at home.

Isaac Watts (1674–1748)

God's Word

He who dwells in the secret place of the Most High
shall abide under the shadow of the Almighty.
I will say of the Lord, "He is my refuge and my fortress;
my God, in Him I will trust."
Surely He shall deliver you from the snare of the fowler
and from the perilous pestilence.
He shall cover you with His feathers,
and under His wings you shall take refuge;
His truth shall be your shield and buckler.
You shall not be afraid of the terror by night,
nor of the arrow that flies by day,
nor of the pestilence that walks in darkness,
nor of the destruction that lays waste at noonday.
A thousand may fall at your side,
and ten thousand at your right hand;
but it shall not come near you.

. . .

Because you have made the Lord, who is my refuge,
even the Most High, your dwelling place,
no evil shall befall you,
nor shall any plague come near your dwelling;
for He shall give His angels charge over you,
to keep you in all your ways.
—Psalm 91:1–7, 9–11

Reflection

Best of all, God is with us.
—John Wesley (1703–1791)

Just When I Need Him Most

Just when I need Him,
Jesus is near.
Just when I falter,
Just when I fear;
Ready to help me,
Ready to cheer,
Just when I need Him most.

Just when I need Him,
Jesus is true.
Never forsaking,
All the way through;
Giving for burdens
Pleasures anew,
Just when I need Him most.

Just when I need Him,
Jesus is strong.
Bearing my burdens
All the day long;
For all my sorrow
Giving a song,
Just when I need Him most.

Just when I need Him,
He is my all.
Answering when
Upon Him I call;
Tenderly watching
Lest I should fall,
Just when I need him most.

William C. Poole (1875–1949)

God's Word

God is our refuge and strength,
a very present help in trouble.
—Psalm 46:1

When you pass through the waters, I will be with you;
and through the rivers, they shall not overflow you.
When you walk through the fire, you shall not be burned,
nor shall the flame scorch you.
For I am the Lord your God.
—Isaiah 43:2–3

O, Lord, You are of my inheritance and my cup;
You maintain my lot.
—Psalm 16:5

Reflection

Doubt not His grace because of thy tribulations,
but believe that He loveth thee
as much in seasons of trouble
as in times of happiness.
—Charles Spurgeon (1834–1892)

He Keeps Me Singing

There's within my heart a melody
Jesus whispers sweet and low;
"Fear not, I am with thee;
Peace be still,"
In all of life's ebb and flow.

All my life was wrecked by sin and strife,
Discord filled my heart with pain;
Jesus swept across the broken strings,
Stirred the slumbering chords again.

Feasting on the riches of His grace,
Resting 'neath His sheltering wings,
Always looking on His smiling face—
That is why I shout and sing.

Though sometimes He leads through waters deep,
Trials fall across the way;
Though sometimes the path seems rough and steep,
See His footprints all the way.

Soon He's coming back to welcome me,
Far beyond the starry sky;
I shall wing my flight to worlds unknown,
I shall reign with Him on high.

Jesus.
Sweetest name I know.
Fills my every longing,
Keeps me singing as I go.

Luther B. Bridgers (1884–1948)

God's Word

Rejoice in the Lord, O you righteous!
For praise from the upright is beautiful.
—Psalm 33:1

And they sang responsively,
Praising and giving thanks to the Lord:
"For He is good, for His mercy endures
forever toward Israel."
—Ezra 3:11

Sing, O heavens!
Be joyful, O earth!
And break out in singing, O mountains!
For the Lord has comforted His people,
and will have mercy on His afflicted.
—Isaiah 49:13

Reflection

As long as we live, there is never enough singing.
—Martin Luther (1483–1546)

Day by Day

Day by day,
And with each passing moment,
Strength I find to meet my trials here.

Just as I Am

Just as I am, though tossed about
With many a conflict,
Many a doubt.

We Have an Anchor

Will your anchor hold in the storms of life,
When the clouds unfold their wings of strife?
When the strong tides lift and the cables strain,
Will your anchor drift, or firm remain?

It is safely moored, 'twill the storm withstand,
For it's well secured by the Savior's hand;
And the cables passed from His heart to mine,
Can defy the blast, through strength divine.

It will firmly hold in the straits of fear,
When the breakers have told the reef is near;
Though the tempest rave and the wild winds blow,
Not an angry wave shall our bark overflow.

It will firmly hold in the Floods of Death—
When the waters cold chill our latest breath;
On the rising tide it can never fail,
While our hopes abide within the Veil.

When our eyes behold through the gathering night
The city of gold, our harbor bright,
We shall anchor fast by the heavenly shore,
With the storms all past forevermore.

We have an anchor that keeps the soul
Steadfast and sure while the billows roll;
Fastened to the rock which cannot move,
Grounded firm and deep in the Savior's love.

Priscilla Jane Owens (1829–1906)

God's Word

This hope we have as an anchor of the soul,
both sure and steadfast.
—Hebrews 6:19

Through the Lord's mercies, we are not consumed,
because His compassions fail not.
They are new every morning;
great is Your faithfulness.
"The Lord is my portion," says my soul,
"therefore, I hope in Him!"
—Lamentations 3:22–24

But the Lord is faithful,
who shall establish you,
and guard you from the evil one.
—2 Thessalonians 3:3

Reflection

God's strength behind you,
His concern for you,
His love within you,
and His arms beneath you
are more than sufficient for the job ahead of you.
—William Arthur Ward (1921–1996)

From Every Stormy Wind That Blows

From every stormy wind that blows,
From every swelling tide of woes,
There is a calm, a sure retreat;
'Tis found beneath the mercy seat.

There is a place where Jesus sheds
The oil of gladness on our heads;
A place than all besides more sweet,
It is the blood-bought mercy seat.

There is a scene where spirits blend,
Where friend holds fellowship with friend,
Though sundered far, by faith they meet
Around one common mercy seat.

Ah, whither could we flee for aid,
When tempted, desolate, dismayed,
Or how the hosts of hell defeat,
Had suffering saints no mercy seat?

There, there, on eagles' wings we soar,
And time and sense seem all no more;
And heaven comes down, our souls to greet,
And glory crowns the mercy seat.

O may my hand forget her skill,
My tongue be silent, cold and still,
This bounding heart forget to beat,
If I forget the mercy seat!

Hugh Stowell (1799–1865)

God's Word

You shall make a mercy seat of pure gold;
two and a half cubits shall be its length
and a cubit and a half its width.

...

And there I will meet with you,
and I will speak with you from above the mercy seat,
from between the two cherubim
which are on the ark of the Testimony.
—Exodus 25:17, 22

The Lord is my light and my salvation;
whom shall I fear?
The Lord is the strength of my life;
of whom shall I be afraid?
—Psalm 27:1

These things I have written to you who believe in the
name of the Son of God,
that you may know that you have eternal life.
—1 John 5:13

Reflection

To every soul that knows how to pray,
that by faith comes to Jesus, the true mercy seat,
God has no dark or terrible aspect but is filled with love.
—Charles Spurgeon (1834–1892)

God Leads Us Along

In shady green pastures, so rich and so sweet,
God leads His dear children along;
Where the water's cool flow bathes the weary one's feet,
God leads His dear children along.

Sometimes on the mount where the sun shines so bright,
God leads His dear children along.
Sometimes in the valley, in the darkest of night,
God leads His dear children along.

Though sorrows befall us and Satan oppose,
God leads His dear children along.
Through grace we can conquer, defeat all our foes;
God leads His dear children along.

Away from the mire, and away from the clay,
God leads His dear children along.
Away up in glory, eternity's day,
God leads His dear children along.

Some through the waters, some through the flood,
Some through the fire, but all through the blood.
Some through great sorrow, but God gives a song
In the night season and all the day long.

George A. Young (1855–1935)

God's Word

The steps of a good man are ordered by the Lord,
and He delights in his way.
Though he fall, he shall not be utterly cast down,
for the Lord upholds him with His hand.
—Psalm 37:23–24

"These things I have spoken to you,
that you should not be made to stumble."
—John 16:1

Show me Your ways, O Lord; teach me Your paths.
Lead me in Your truth and teach me,
for You are the God of my salvation;
on You I wait all the day.
—Psalm 25:4–5

Reflection

Never be afraid to trust an unknown future
to a known God.
—Corrie ten Boom (1892–1983)

Just as I Am

Just as I am, without one plea,
But that Thy blood was shed for me;
And that Thou bidst me come to Thee,
O Lamb of God, I come.

Just as I am, and waiting not
To rid my soul of one dark blot;
To Thee, whose blood can cleanse each spot,
O Lamb of God, I come.

Just as I am, though tossed about
With many a conflict, many a doubt;
Fightings and fears within, without,
O Lamb of God, I come.

Just as I am—poor, wretched, blind;
Sight, riches, healing of the mind—
Yes, all I need in Thee to find,
O Lamb of God, I come.

Just as I am, Thou will receive,
Will welcome, pardon, cleanse, relieve;
Because Thy promise I believe,
O Lamb of God, I come.

Just as I am—Thy love unknown,
Has broken every barrier down;
Now to be Thine, yes, Thine alone,
O Lamb of God, I come.

Just as I am, of that free love,
The breadth, length, depth and height to prove;
Here for a season, then above,
O Lamb of God, I come.

Charlotte Elliott (1789–1871)

God's Word

"The one who comes to Me
I will by no means cast out."
—John 6:37

For all have sinned
and fall short of the glory of God.
—Romans 3:23

Jesus said to him, "If you can believe,
all things are possible to him who believes."
Immediately the father of the child cried out,
and said with tears,
"Lord, I believe; help my unbelief!"
—Mark 9:23–24

This is a faithful saying and worthy of all acceptance,
that Christ Jesus came into the world to save sinners,
of whom I am chief.
—1 Timothy 1:15

Reflection

Humility is the virtue by which a man recognizes
his own unworthiness because he truly knows himself.
—Bernard of Clairvaux (1090–1153)

Living by Faith

I care not today what tomorrow may bring,
If shadow or sunshine or rain;
The Lord I know ruleth over everything
And all of my worry is vain.

Though tempests may blow, and the storm clouds arise,
Obscuring the brightness of life,
I'm never alarmed at the overcast skies—
The Master looks on at the strife.

I know that He safely will carry me through,
No matter what evils betide;
Why should I then care, though the tempest may blow,
If Jesus walks close to my side?

Our Lord will return to this earth some sweet day,
Our troubles will then all be over;
The Master so gently will lead us away,
Beyond that blessed heavenly shore.

Living by faith, in Jesus above,
Trusting, confiding in His great love.
Safe from all harm in His sheltering arms,
I'm living by faith and feel no alarm.

James Wells, v. 1–3 (ca. 1918), biography unknown
—Robert E. Winsett, v. 4 (1876–1952)

God's Word

Therefore, we do not lose heart.
Even though our outward man is perishing,
yet the inward man is being renewed day by day.
For our light affliction, which is but for a moment,
is working for us a far more exceeding and eternal weight of glory,
while we do not look at the things which are seen,
but at the things which are not seen.
For the things which are seen are temporary,
but the things which are not seen are eternal.
—2 Corinthians 4:16–18

Now faith is the substance of things hoped for,
the evidence of things not seen.
For by it the elders obtained a good testimony.
—Hebrews 11:1–2

So then faith comes by hearing,
and hearing by the Word of God.
—Romans 10:17

Reflection

This is our Lord's will—
that our prayers and our faith be alike.
Large.
—Julian of Norwich (1342–1416)

Joyful, Joyful, We Adore Thee

Joyful, joyful, we adore Thee,
God of glory, Lord of love;
Hearts unfold like flowers before Thee, opening to the sun above.
Melt the clouds of sin and sadness, drive the dark of doubt away;
Giver of immortal gladness,
Fill us with the light of day.

All Thy works with joy surrounds Thee,
Earth and heaven reflect Thy rays,
Stars and angels sing around Thee, center of unbroken praise.
Field and forest, vale and mountain, flowery meadow, flashing sea,
Singing bird and flowing fountain
Call us to rejoice in Thee.

Thou art giving and forgiving,
Ever blessing, ever blessed,
Wellspring of the joy of living, ocean depth of happy rest.
Thou our Father, Christ and Brother, all who live in love are Thine;
Teach us how to love each other,
Lift us to the joy divine.

Mortals join the happy chorus
Which the morning stars began;
Father love is reigning over us, brother love binds man to man.
Ever singing, march we onward, victors in the midst of strife.
Joyful music leads us sunward
In the triumph song of life.

Henry van Dyke (1852–1933)

God's Word

Sing to the Lord, all the earth;
proclaim the good news of His salvation from day to day.
Declare His glory among the nations,
His wonders among all peoples.
—1 Chronicles 16:23–24

The Lord lives!
Blessed be my Rock!
Let God be exalted,
the Rock of my salvation!

. . .

Therefore, I will give thanks to You,
O Lord, among the Gentiles,
and sing praises to Your name.
—2 Samuel 22:47, 50

Praise the Lord, call upon His name;
declare His deeds among the peoples,
make mention that His name is exalted.
Sing to the Lord,
for He has done excellent things; . . .
Cry out and shout, O inhabitant of Zion,
for great is the Holy One of Israel in your midst!
—Isaiah 12:4–6

Reflection

May God protect me from gloomy saints.
—Saint Teresa of Avila (1515–1582)

Day by Day

Day by day, and with each passing moment,
Strength I find to meet my trials here.
Trusting in my Father's wise bestowment,
I've no cause for worry or for fear.

He whose heart is kind beyond all measure
Gives unto each day what He deems best—
Lovingly, it's part of pain and pleasure,
Mingling toil with peace and rest.

Every day the Lord Himself is near me
With a special mercy for each hour.
All my cares He fain would bear, and cheer me,
He whose Name is Counselor and Power,

The protection of His child and treasure
Is a charge that on Himself He laid;
"As thy days, thy strength shall be in measure,"
This the pledge to me He made.

Help me then in every tribulation,
So to trust Thy promises, O Lord,
That I lose not faith's sweet consolation
Offered me within Thy holy Word.

Help me, Lord, when toil and trouble meeting,
E'er to take, as from a father's hand,
One by one, the days, the moments fleeting,
'Til I reach that promised land.

Karolina W. Sandell-Berg (1832–1903)
Translated from Swedish to English by A. L. Skoog (1856–1934)

God's Word

I can do all things through Christ
who strengthens me.
—Philippians 4:13

Have you not known? Have you not heard?
The everlasting God, the Lord,
the Creator of the ends of the earth,
neither faints nor is weary.
His understanding is unsearchable.
He gives power to the weak,
and to those who have no might, He increases strength.
—Isaiah 40:28–29

Finally, my brethren, be strong in the Lord
and in the power of His might.
Put on the whole armor of God,
that you may be able to stand against
the wiles of the devil.
—Ephesians 6:10–11

Reflection

Out of our suffering comes the serious mind;
out of salvation, the grateful heart;
out of endurance, fortitude;
out of deliverance, faith.
Patient endurance attends to all things.
—Saint Teresa of Avila (1515–1582)

Leaning on the Everlasting Arms

What a fellowship,
What a joy divine!
What a blessedness,
What a peace is mine,
Leaning on the everlasting arms.

Oh, how sweet to walk,
In this pilgrim way!
Oh, how bright the path
Grows from day to day,
Leaning on the everlasting arms.

What have I to dread,
What have I to fear?
I have blessed peace
With my Lord so near,
Leaning on the everlasting arms.

Leaning,
Safe and secure from all alarm.
Leaning,
On the everlasting arms.

Elisha A. Hoffman (1839–1929)

God's Word

The eternal God is your refuge,
and underneath are the everlasting arms;
He will thrust out the enemy from before you,
and will say, "Destroy!"
—Deuteronomy 33:27

Even to your old age, I am He,
and even to gray hairs I will carry you!
I have made, and I will bear;
even I will carry, and will deliver you.
—Isaiah 46:4

Lord, You have been our dwelling place in all generations.
Before the mountains were brought forth,
or ever You had formed the earth and the world,
even from everlasting to everlasting,
You are God!
—Psalm 90:1–2

Reflection

Jesus came treading the waves;
and so, He puts all the swelling tumults of life under His feet.
Christians—why afraid?
—Saint Augustine (354–430)

Turn Your Eyes upon Jesus

O Soul, are you weary and troubled?
No light in the darkness you see?
There's a light for a look at the Savior,
And life more abundant and free.

Through death into life everlasting
He passed, and we follow Him there.
Over us sin no more hath dominion—
For more than conquerors we are!

His Word shall not fail you, He promised;
Believe Him, and all will be well.
Then go to a world that is dying,
His perfect salvation to tell.

Turn your eyes upon Jesus,
Look full in His wonderful face,
And the things of earth will grow strangely dim,
In the light of His glory and grace.

Helen H. Lemmel (1863–1961)

God's Word

Looking unto Jesus,
the author and finisher of our faith,
who for the joy that was set before Him
endured the cross, despising the shame,
and has sat down at the right hand of the throne of God.
—Hebrews 12:2

I sought the Lord, and He heard me,
and delivered me from all my fears.
They looked to Him and were radiant,
and their faces were not ashamed.
This poor man cried out, and the Lord heard him
and saved him out of all his troubles.
—Psalm 34:4–6

But he, being full of the Holy Spirit,
gazed into heaven and saw the glory of God,
And Jesus standing at the right hand of God.
—Acts 7:55

Reflection

Seek Christ, and you will find Him,
and with him everything else thrown in.
—C. S. Lewis (1898–1963)

I Will Make the Darkness Light

I will make the darkness light before thee,
What is wrong I'll make it right before thee,
All thy battles I will fight before thee,
And the high place I'll bring down.

With an everlasting love I'll love thee,
Though with trials deep and sore I'll prove thee,
But there's nothing that can hurt or move thee,
And the high place I'll bring down.

Although Satan in his rage would tear thee,
And with all his winning arts would snare thee,
Even down to thine old age I'll bear thee,
And the high place I'll bring down.

I will make the darkness light before thee,
I will make the crooked straight before thee,
I will spread My wings protecting over thee,
And the high place I'll bring down.

When thou walkest by the way I'll lead thee,
On the fatness of the land I'll feed thee,
A mansion in the sky I'll deed thee,
And the high place I'll bring down.

Charles P. Jones (1865–1949)

God's Word

The people who walked in darkness
have seen a great light;
those who dwelt in the land of the shadow of death,
upon them a light has shined.
—Isaiah 9:2

Through the tender mercy of our God,
with which the Dayspring from on high has visited us;
to give light to those who sit in darkness
and the shadow of death,
to guide our feet into the way of peace.
—Luke 1:69

Then Jesus spoke to them again, saying,
"I am the Light of the world.
He who follows Me shall not walk in darkness
but have the Light of life."
—John 8:12

Reflection

If I forget that it was He
who granted that ray of light to His servant,
then, I know nothing of Calvary love.
—Amy Carmichael (1867–1951)

What a Friend We Have in Jesus

Are we weak and heavy laden,
Cumbered with a load of care?
Precious Savior, still our refuge—
Take it to the Lord in prayer.

Hold to God's Unchanging Hand

Time is filled with swift transition,
Naught of earth unmoved can stand.
Build your hopes on things eternal;
Hold to God's unchanging hand.

Wonderful Peace

Far away in the depths of my spirit tonight
Rolls a melody sweeter than psalm;
In celestial-like strains it unceasingly falls
Over my soul like an infinite calm.

What a treasure I have in this wonderful peace,
Buried deep in the heart of my soul;
So secure that no power can mine it away,
While the years of eternity roll.

I am resting tonight in this wonderful peace,
Resting sweetly in Jesus' control;
For I'm kept from all danger by night and by day,
And His glory is flooding my soul.

And I know when I rise to that city of peace,
Where the Author of peace I shall see,
That one strain of the anthems the ransomed will sing
In that heavenly kingdom will be.

O soul, are you here without comfort or rest,
Walking down the rough pathway of time?
Make Jesus your friend ere the shadows grow dark;
O accept this sweet peace so sublime.

Peace, peace,
Wonderful peace.
Coming down from the Father above.
Sweep over my spirit forever, I pray
In fathomless billows of love.

Warren Donald Cornell (1858–1930s?)

God's Word

Let the peace of God rule in your hearts,
to which also you were called in one body;
and be thankful.
—Colossians 3:15

Be anxious in nothing,
but in everything by prayer and supplication,
with thanksgiving, let your requests be made known to God;
and the peace of God,
which surpasses all understanding,
will guard your hearts and minds through Christ Jesus.
—Philippians 4:6–7

Great peace have those who love Your law,
and nothing causes them to stumble.
—Psalm 119:165

Reflection

And I smiled to think God's greatness
flowed around our incompleteness,
round our restlessness, His rest.
—Elizabeth Barrett Browning (1806–1861)

His Eye Is on the Sparrow

Why should I feel discouraged?
Why should the shadows come?
Why should my heart be lonely
And long for heaven and home?
When Jesus is my portion, ·
My constant friend is He;
His eye is on the sparrow,
And I know He watches.

"Let not your heart be troubled,"
His tender Word I hear,
And resting on His goodness,
I lose my doubts and fears;
Though by the path He leadeth,
But one step I may see;
His eye is on the sparrow,
And I know He watches me.

Whenever I am tempted,
Whenever clouds arise,
When songs give place to sighing,
When hope within me dies—
I draw the closer to Him,
From care He sets me free;
His eye is on the sparrow,
And I know He watches me.

I sing because I'm happy!
I sing because I'm free!
His eye is on the sparrow,
And I know He watches me.

Civilla D. Martin (1866–1948)

God's Word

Are not two sparrows sold for a copper coin?
And not one of them falls to the ground
apart from your Father's will.
But the very hairs on your head are all numbered.
Do not fear therefore;
you are of more value than many sparrows.
—Matthew 10:29–30

But now ask the beasts, and they will teach you;
and the birds of the air, and they will tell you;
or speak to the earth, and it will teach you;
and the fish of the sea will explain to you.
Who among all these does not know
that the hand of the Lord has done this,
in whose hand is the life of every living thing.
—Job 12:7–10

Let not your heart be troubled;
You believe in God, believe also in Me.
—John 14:1

Reflection

Oh, God,
Thy sea is so great,
and my boat is so small.
—Breton Fisherman's Prayer

My Faith Has Found a Resting Place

My faith has found a resting place,
Not in device or creed;
I trust the ever living One,
His wounds for me shall plead.

Enough for me that Jesus saves,
This ends my fear and doubt;
A sinful soul I come to Him,
He'll never cast me out.

My heart is leaning on the Word,
The living Word of God;
Salvation by my Savior's Name,
Salvation through His blood.

My great Physician heals the sick,
The lost He came to save;
For me His precious blood He shed,
For me His life He gave.

I need no other argument,
I need no other plea;
It is enough that Jesus died,
And that He died for me.

Eliza Edmunds Hewitt (1851–1920)

God's Word

There are many who say,
"Who will show us any good?"
Lord, lift up the light of Your countenance upon us.
You have put gladness in my heart,
more than in the season that their grain and wine increased.
I will both lie down in peace, and sleep;
for You alone, O Lord, make me dwell in safety.
—Psalm 4:6–8

My Son, let them not depart from your eyes—
keep sound wisdom and discretion;
so they will be life to your soul
and grace to your neck.
Then you will walk safely in your way,
And your foot will not stumble.
When you lie down, you will not be afraid;
yes, when you lie down, your sleep will be sweet.
—Proverbs 3:21–24

Reflection

God cannot give us happiness and peace
apart from Himself because it is not there.
There is no such thing.
—C. S. Lewis (1898–1963)

What a Friend We Have in Jesus

What a friend we have in Jesus,
All our sins and griefs to bear;
What a privilege to carry
Everything to God in prayer.

O what peace we often forfeit,
O what needless pain we bear;
All because we do not carry
Everything to God in prayer.

Have we trials and temptations?
Is there trouble anywhere?
We should never be discouraged,
Take it to the Lord in prayer.

Can we find a friend so faithful,
Who will all our sorrows share?
Jesus knows our every weakness;
Take it to the Lord in prayer.

Are we weak and heavy laden,
Cumbered with a load of care?
Precious Savior, still our refuge—
Take it to the Lord in prayer.

Do thy friends despise, forsake you?
Take it to the Lord in prayer.
In His arms He'll take and shield you,
Thou will find a solace there.

Joseph M. Scriven (1819–1886)

God's Word

"Come to Me, all you who labor and
are heavy laden, and I will give you rest.
Take My yoke upon you and learn from Me,
for I am gentle and lowly in heart,
and you will find rest for your souls.
For My yoke is easy and My burden is light."
—Matthew 11:28–30

Draw near to God, and He will draw near to you. …
Humble yourselves in the sight of the Lord,
And He will lift you up.
—James 4:8, 10

"No longer do I call you servants,
for a servant does not know what his master is doing;
but I have called you friends,
for all things that I heard from My Father,
I have made known to you."
—John 15:15

Reflection

I have read in Plato and Cicero sayings which are
very wise and very beautiful;
but I have never read in either of them:
"Come unto Me all ye that labor and are heavy laden."
—Saint Augustine (354–430)

Hold to God's Unchanging Hand

Time is filled with swift transition,
Naught of earth unmoved can stand.
Build your hopes on things eternal;
Hold to God's unchanging hand.

Trust in Him who will not leave you,
Whatsoever years may bring.
If by earthly friends forsaken,
Still more closely to Him cling.

Covet not this world's vain riches
That so rapidly decay.
Seek to gain the heavenly treasures;
They will never pass away.

When your journey is completed,
If to God you have been true,
Fair and bright the home in glory
Your enraptured soul will view.

Build your hopes on things eternal.
Hold to God's unchanging hand.

Jennie Bain Wilson (1856–1913)

God's Word

For I am the Lord, I do not change;
therefore you are not consumed, O sons of Jacob.
—Malachi 3:6

Jesus Christ is the same yesterday
today, and forever.
—Hebrews 13:8

Then to Him was given dominion
and glory and a kingdom,
that all peoples, nations, and languages should serve Him.
His dominion is an everlasting dominion,
which shall not pass away,
and His kingdom the one
which shall not be destroyed.
—Daniel 7:14

Reflection

Have courage for the great sorrows of life
and patience for the small ones;
and when you have laboriously accomplished your daily task,
go to sleep in peace.
God is awake.
—Victor Hugo (1802–1885)

Abide with Me

Abide with me; fast falls the eventide,
The darkness deepens, Lord, with me abide.
When other helpers fail and comforts flee,
Help of the helpless, O abide with me.

Thou on my head in early youth did smile,
And though rebellious and perverse meanwhile,
Thou hast not left me, oft as I left Thee.
On to the close, O Lord, abide with me.

I need Thy presence every passing hour.
What but Thy grace can foil the tempter's power?
Who, like Thyself, my guide and stay can be?
Through cloud and sunshine, Lord, abide with me.

I fear no foe, with Thee at hand to bless;
Ills have no weight and tears no bitterness.
Where is death's sting? Where, grave, thy victory?
I triumph still if Thou abide with me.

Hold Thou Thy cross before my closing eyes;
Shine through the gloom and point me to the skies.
Heaven's morning breaks, and earth's vain shadows flee,
In life, in death, O Lord, abide with me.

Henry Francis Lyte (1793–1847)

God's Word

God is our refuge and strength,
a very present help in trouble.
Therefore, we will not fear,
even though the earth be removed,
and though the mountains be carried into the midst of the sea;
—Psalm 46:1–2

"If you abide in Me, and My Words abide in you,
you will ask what you desire, and it shall be done for you. ...
If you keep My commandments,
you will abide in My love;
just as I have kept My Father's commandments
and abide in His love."
—John 15:7, 10

The Lord your God is in your midst,
the Mighty One, will save;
He will rejoice over you with gladness,
He will quiet you with His love,
He will rejoice over you with singing.
—Zephaniah 3:17

Reflection

Abide in peace, banish cares,
take no account of all that happened,
and you will serve God according His good pleasure
and rest in Him.
—Saint John of the Cross (1542–1591)

Standing on the Promises

Standing on the promises of Christ, my King;
Through eternal ages, let His praises ring.
Glory in the highest, I will shout and sing,
Standing on the promises of God.

Standing on the promises that cannot fail,
When the howling storms of doubt and fear assail;
By the living word of God, I shall prevail,
Standing on the promises of God.

Standing on the promises, I now can see
Perfect, present cleansing in the blood for me.
Standing in the liberty where Christ makes free,
Standing on the promises of God.

Standing on the promises of Christ the Lord,
Bound to Him eternally by love's strong cord.
Overcoming daily with the Spirit's sword,
Standing on the promises of God.

Standing on the promises, I cannot fall,
Listening every moment to the Spirit's call.
Resting in my Savior as my all in all,
Standing on the promises of God.

Russell Kelso Carter (1849–1928)

God's Word

Watch, stand fast in the faith,
be brave, be strong.
Let all that you do
be done with love.
—1 Corinthians 16:13

Therefore take up the whole armor of God,
that you may be able to withstand in the evil day,
and having done all, to stand.
—Ephesians 6:13

And Moses said to the people,
"Do not be afraid.
Stand still, and see the salvation of the Lord,
which He will accomplish for you today."
—Exodus 14:13

Reflection

Be sure you put your feet in the right place,
then stand firm.
—Abraham Lincoln (1809–1865)

Be Thou My Vision

Be Thou my vision, O Lord of my heart;
Naught be all else to me, save that Thou art.
Thou my best thought, by day or by night;
Waking or sleeping, Thy presence my light.

Be Thou my wisdom, and Thou my true Word;
I ever with Thee and Thou with me, Lord.
Thou my great Father, I Thy true son;
Thou in me dwelling and I with Thee one.

Be Thou my battle shield, sword for my fight;
Be Thou my dignity, Thou my delight.
Thou my soul's shelter, Thou my high tower;
Raise Thou me heavenward, O Power of my power.

Riches I heed not, nor man's empty praise,
Thou mine inheritance, now and always.
Thou and Thou only, first in my heart,
High King of heaven, my treasure Thou art.

High King of heaven, my victory won,
May I reach heaven's joys, bright heaven's Sun?
Heart of my own heart, whatever befall,
Still be my vision, O Ruler of all.

Old Irish hymn attributed to Dallan Forgail (530–598)
Translated to English by Mary Elizabeth Byrne (1880–1931)

God's Word

Thus says the Lord,
"Let not the wise man glory of his wisdom,
let not the mighty man glory in his might,
nor let the rich man glory in his riches;
but let him who glories glory in this,
that he understands and knows Me,
that I am the Lord, exercising lovingkindness,
justice and righteousness on earth;
for in these I delight," declares the Lord.
—Jeremiah 9:23–24

Set your mind on the things above,
not on the things that are on earth.
—Colossians 3:2

"If that is the case, our God whom we serve
is able to deliver us from the burning, fiery furnace,
and He will deliver us from your hand, O king.
But, if not, let it be known to you,
O king, that we do not serve your gods,
nor will we worship the gold image which you have set up."
—Daniel 3:17

Reflection

The world appears very little to a soul
that contemplates the greatness of God.
—Brother Lawrence (1614–1691)

'Tis So Sweet to Trust in Jesus

'Tis so sweet to trust in Jesus,
Just to take Him at His Word;
Just to rest upon His promise,
And to know, "Thus saith the Lord."

O, how sweet to trust in Jesus,
Just to trust His cleansing blood,
And in simple faith to plunge me,
'Neath the healing, cleansing flood.

Yes, 'tis sweet to trust in Jesus,
Just from sin and self to cease,
Just from Jesus simply taking
Life and rest, joy and peace.

I'm so glad I learned to trust Thee,
Precious Jesus, Savior, Friend.
And I know that Thou art with me,
Will be with me to the end.

Jesus, how I trust Him!
How I've proved Him o'er and o'er.
Jesus, precious Jesus,
O, for grace to trust Him more.

Louisa Stead (1850–1917)

God's Word

And those who know Your name
will put their trust in You;
for You, Lord, have not forsaken those who seek You.
—Psalm 9:10

Do not be wise in your own eyes;
fear the Lord and depart from evil.
It will be health to your flesh,
and strength to your bones.
—Proverbs 3:7–8

The King was exceedingly glad for him,
and commanded that they should take Daniel up out of the den.
So Daniel was taken up out of the den
and no injury whatever was found on him,
because he believed in his God.
—Daniel 6:23

Whenever I am afraid, I will trust in You.
—Psalm 56:3

Reflection

How sweet the Name of Jesus sounds in a believer's ear!
It soothes his sorrows,
heals his wounds and drives away his fears.
—John Newton (1725–1807)

Our (O) God, Our Help in Ages Past

O, God, our help in ages past,
Our hope for years to come;
Our shelter from the stormy blast,
And our eternal home.

Under the shadow of Thy throne,
Thy saints have dwelt secure;
Sufficient is Thine arm alone,
And our defense is sure.

Before the hills in order stood,
Or earth received her frame,
From everlasting Thou art God,
To endless years the same.

A thousand ages in Thy sight
Are like an evening gone;
Short as the watch that ends the night
Before the rising sun.

Time, like an ever-rolling stream,
Bears all its sons away;
They fly, forgotten, as a dream
Dies at the opening day.

O, God, our help in ages past,
Our hope for years to come,
Be Thou our guard while life shall last,
And our eternal home.

Isaac Watts (1674–1748)
Note: John Wesley changed "Our God" to "O God" (ca. 1738).

God's Word

I am the Alpha and the Omega,
the Beginning and the End,
the First and the Last.
—Revelation 22:13

Remember to magnify His work,
Of which men have sung.
Everyone has seen it;
Man looks on it from afar.
Behold, God is great,
and we do not know Him;
Nor can the number of His years be discovered.
—Job 36:24–26

Who has performed and done it,
calling the generations from the beginning?
I, the Lord, am the first;
and with the last I am He.
—Isaiah 41:4

Reflection

We may ignore,
but we can nowhere evade the presence of God.
The world is crowded with Him.
He walks everywhere incognito.
—C. S. Lewis (1898–1963)

My Faith Looks Up To Thee

May Thy rich grace impart
Strength to my fainting heart,
My zeal inspire.

O Jesus, I Have Promised

I shall not fear the battle if Thou art by my side,
Nor wander from the pathway
If Thou will be my guide.

The Unclouded Day

O they tell me of a home far beyond the skies,
O they tell me of a home far away;
O they tell me of a home where no storm clouds rise,
O they tell me of an uncloudy day.

O they tell me of a home where my friends have gone,
O they tell me of that land far away;
Where the tree of life in eternal bloom
Sheds its fragrance through the uncloudy day.

O they tell me of a King in His beauty there,
And they tell me that mine eyes shall behold
Where He sits on the throne that is whiter than snow,
In the city that is made of gold.

O they tell me that He smiles on His children there,
And His smile drives their sorrows all away;
And they tell me that no tears ever come again,
In the lovely land of uncloudy day.

O the land of cloudless days,
O the land of an unclouded sky;
O they tell me of a home where no storm clouds rise,
O they tell me of an unclouded day.

Josiah Kelley Alwood (1828–1909)

God's Word

But now they desire a better,
that is, a heavenly country.
Therefore God is not ashamed
to be called their God,
for He has prepared a city for them.
—Hebrews 11:16

We are confident, yes,
well pleased rather to be absent
from the body and to be present
with the Lord.
—2 Corinthians 5:8

For here we have no continuing city,
but we seek the one to come.
—Hebrews 13:14

Reflection

A continual looking forward to the eternal world
is not a form of escapism or wishful thinking,
but one of the things a Christian is meant to do.
—C. S. Lewis (1898–1963)

O Jesus, I Have Promised

O Jesus, I have promised to serve Thee to the end;
Be Thou forever near me, my Master and my Friend.
I shall not fear the battle if Thou art by my side,
Nor wander from the pathway if Thou will be my guide.

O let me feel Thee near me, the world is ever near;
I see the sights that dazzle, the tempting sounds I hear.
My foes are ever near me, around me and within;
But Jesus, draw Thou nearer, and shield my soul from sin.

O let me hear Thee speaking in accents clear and still,
Above the storms of passion, the murmurs of self will.
O speak to reassure me, to hasten or control!
O speak and make me listen, Thou guardian of my soul.

O Jesus, Thou hast promised to all who follow Thee,
That where Thou art in glory there shall Thy servant be.
And, Jesus, I have promised to serve Thee to the end,
O give me grace to follow, my Master and my Friend.

O let me see Thy foot-mark, and in them plant my own;
My hope to follow duly is in Thy strength alone.
O guide me, call me, draw me, uphold me to the end.
At last in heaven receive me, my Savior and my Friend.

John E. Bode (1816–1874)

God's Word

You shall walk in all the ways
which the Lord your God has commanded you,
that you may live and that it may be well with you
and that you may prolong your days
in the land which you shall possess.
—Deuteronomy 5:33

Then Jesus said to His disciples,
"If anyone desires to come after Me,
let him deny himself,
and take up his cross, and follow Me."
—Matthew 16:24

Blessed are all who fear the Lord,
who walk in obedience to Him.
—Psalm 128:1

Reflection

When I stand before God at the end of my life,
I hope that I won't have a single bit of talent left—
and can say, "I used up everything You gave me."
—Erma Bombeck (1927–1996)

Sweetly Resting

In the rifted Rock, I'm resting,
Safely sheltered, I abide.
There no foes nor storms molest me,
While within the cleft I hide.

Long pursued by sin and Satan,
Weary, sad, I longed for rest.
Then I found this heavenly shelter,
Opened in my Savior's breast.

Peace which passeth understanding,
Joy the world can never give,
Now in Jesus I am finding;
In His smiles of love I live.

In the rifted rock I'll hide me
Till the storms of life are past;
All secure in this blest refuge,
Heeding not the fiercest blast.

Now I'm resting, sweetly resting,
In the cleft once made for me.
Jesus, blessed Rock of Ages,
I will hide myself in Thee.

Mary Dagworthy James (1810–1883)

God's Word

Then you will walk safely in your way,
and your foot will not stumble.
When you lie down, you will not be afraid;
yes, you will lie down and your sleep will be sweet.
Do not be afraid of sudden terror,
nor of trouble from the wicked when it comes;
for the Lord will be your confidence,
and will keep your foot from being caught.
—Proverbs 3:23–26

Then Moses said to the Lord, …
"Now, therefore,
I pray, if I have found grace in Your sight,
show me now Your way,
that I may know You and that I may find grace in Your sight.
And consider that this nation is Your people."
And He said, "My Presence will go with you,
and I will give you rest."
—Exodus 33:12, 13–14

Reflection

Daniel slept in the lion's den,
Peter slept in prison,
Jesus slept in the storm.
Sometimes, no matter your trouble,
It's good to take a nap.
—Unknown

Open My Eyes, That I May See

Open my eyes, that I may see
Glimpses of truth Thou hast for me;
Place in my hands the wonderful key
That shall unclasp and set me free.

Open my ears, that I may hear
Voices of truth Thou sendest clear;
And while the wave notes fall on my ear,
Everything false will disappear.

Open my mind, that I may read
More of Thy love in word and deed;
What shall I fear while yet Thou do lead?
Only for light from Thee I plead.

Open my mouth, and let me bear,
Gladly the warm truth everywhere;
Open my heart and let me prepare
Love with Thy children thus to share.

Silently now I wait for Thee,
Ready my God, Thy will to see.
Open my eyes, ears and heart,
Illumine me, Spirit Divine.

Clara H. Scott (1841–1897)

God's Word

Open Thou my eyes, that I may behold
wondrous things out of Thy law.
—Psalm 119:18

The eyes of your understanding being enlightened;
that you may know
what is the hope of His calling,
what are the riches of the glory of His inheritance in the saints
and what is the exceeding greatness
of His power toward us who believe.
—Ephesians 1:18–19

Now the word of the Lord came to me, saying;
"Son of man, you dwell in the midst of a rebellious house,
which has eyes to see but does not see,
and ears to hear but does not hear;
for they are a rebellious house."
—Ezekiel 12:1–2

Reflection

May the strength of God pilot us.
May the wisdom of God instruct us.
May the hand of God protect us.
May the word of God direct us.
—Saint Patrick (?–461)

My Burdens Rolled Away

I remember when my burdens rolled away;
I had carried them for years, night and day.
When I sought the blessed Lord,
And I took Him at His word,
Then at once all my burdens rolled away.

I remember when my burdens rolled away;
That I feared would never leave, night or day.
Jesus showed to me the loss,
So I left them at the cross;
I was glad that my burdens rolled away.

I remember when my burdens rolled away,
They had hindered me for years, night and day.
As I sought the throne of grace,
Just a glimpse of Jesus' face,
And I knew that my burdens could not stay.

I am singing since my burdens rolled away;
There's a song within my heart, night and day.
I am living for my King,
And with joy, I shout and sing,
"Hallelujah, all my burdens rolled away!"

Minnie A. Steele (first appeared in hymnbooks ca. 1908)

God's Word

Is this not the fast that I have chosen:
to loose the bonds of wickedness,
to undo the heavy burdens,
to let the oppressed go free,
and that you break every yoke?
—Isaiah 58:6

Cast your burden on the Lord,
and He shall sustain you;
He shall never permit the righteous to be moved.
—Psalm 55:22

The righteous cry out, and the Lord hears,
and delivers them out of all their troubles.
—Psalm 34:17

Reflection

Give me a stout heart to bear my own burdens.
Give me a willing heart to bear the burdens of others.
And give me a believing heart to cast
all my burdens upon Thee, O Lord.
—John Baillie (1886–1960)

Higher Ground

I'm pressing on the upward way,
New heights I'm gaining every day;
Still praying as I'm onward bound,
"Lord, plant my feet on higher ground."

My heart has no desire to stay
Where doubts arise and fears dismay;
Though some may dwell where those abound,
My prayer, my aim, is higher ground.

I want to live above the world,
Though Satan's darts at me are hurled,
For faith has caught the joyful sound,
The song of saints on higher ground.

I want to scale the utmost height
And catch a gleam of glory bright;
But still I'll pray 'til heaven I've found,
"Lord, plant my feet on higher ground."

Lord, lift me up and let me stand,
By faith, on heaven's tableland.
A higher plane than I have found,
Lord, plant my feet on higher ground.

Johnson Oatman Jr. (1856–1922)

God's Word

The Lord God is my strength;
He will make my feet like deer's feet,
and He will make me walk on my high hills.
—Habakkuk 3:19

Brothers, I do not count myself to have apprehended;
but one thing I do,
forgetting those things which are behind
and reaching forward to those things which are ahead,
I press toward the goal for the prize
of the upward call of God in Christ Jesus.
—Philippians 3:13–14

And whatever you do,
do it heartily, as to the Lord
and not to men.
—Colossians 3:23

Reflection

Start by doing what is necessary;
then do what is possible;
and suddenly you are doing the impossible.
—Saint Francis of Assisi (1181-1228)

My Faith Looks Up to Thee

My faith looks up to Thee,
Thou Lamb of Calvary,
Savior divine;
Now hear me while I pray,
Take all my guilt away,
O let me from this day be wholly Thine.

May Thy rich grace impart
Strength to my fainting heart,
My zeal inspire.
As Thou hast died for me,
O may my love for Thee,
Pure, warm and changeless be, a living fire.

While life's dark maze I tread,
And griefs around me spread,
Be Thou my guide.
Bid darkness turn to day,
Wipe sorrow's tears away,
Nor let me ever stray from Thee aside.

When ends life's transient dream,
When death's cold sullen stream
Shall over me roll;
Blessed Savior, then in love,
Fear and distrust remove,
O bear me safe above a ransomed soul.

Ray Palmer (1808–1887)

God's Word

Be strong and of good courage,
do not fear nor be afraid of them;
for the Lord your God, He is the One who goes with you.
He will not leave you nor forsake you.
—Deuteronomy 31:6

Fear not, for I am with you;
be not dismayed, for I am your God.
I will strengthen you,
yes, I will help you,
I will uphold you with My right hand.
—Isaiah 41:10

"Peace I leave with you,
My peace I give to you;
not as the world gives do I give to you.
Let not your heart be troubled, neither let it be afraid."
—John 14:27

Reflection

Eight young Christian soldiers,
preparing for a major battle during the Civil War, met in a tent to pray.
They each included the last stanza of this hymn
in letters written to their families that evening.
The next day, seven of them were killed in battle.
—From *A Treasury of Hymns*[1]

---

[1] Amos R. Wells, ed., *A Treasury of Hymns* (Boston: United Society of Christian Endeavor), 1914.

Every Bridge Is Burned Behind Me

Since I started out to find Thee,
Since I to the cross did flee,
Every bridge is burned behind me;
I will never turn from Thee.

Thou did hear my plea so kindly,
Thou did grant me so much grace.
Every bridge is burned behind me;
I will never my steps retrace.

Cares of life perplex and grind me,
Yet I keep the narrow way.
Every bridge is burned behind me;
I from Thee will never stray.

All in all, I ever find Thee,
Savior, Lover, Brother, Friend.
Every bridge is burned behind me;
I will serve Thee to the end.

Strengthen all the ties that bind me,
Closer, closer, Lord to Thee.
Every bridge is burned behind me;
Thine I ever more will be.

Johnson Oatman Jr. (1856–1922)

God's Word

And do not turn aside;
for then you would go after empty things
which cannot profit or deliver, for they are nothing.
For the Lord will not forsake His people,
for His great name's sake,
because it has pleased the Lord to make you His people.
—1 Samuel 12:21–22

Do not love the world or the things in the world.
If anyone loves the world, the love of the Father is not in him.
For all that is in the world—the lust of the flesh,
the lust of the eyes, and the pride of life—
is not of the Father but is of the world.
And the world is passing away,
and the lust of it;
but he who does the will of God abides forever.
—1 John 2:15–17

There are many plans in a man's heart,
nevertheless the Lord's counsel—that will stand.
—Proverbs 19:21

Reflection

The terrible thing, the almost impossible thing,
is to hand over your whole self—all your
wishes and precautions—to Christ.
—C. S. Lewis (1898–1963)

I Love Thy Kingdom, Lord

I love Thy kingdom, Lord;
The house of Thine abode.
The church our blessed Redeemer saved
With His own precious blood.

I love Thy church, O God.
Her walls before Thee stand,
Dear as the apple of Thine eye.
And graven on Thy hand.

For her my tears shall fall,
For her my prayers ascend.
To her my cares and toils given,
Till toils and cares shall end.

Beyond my highest joy,
I prize her heavenly ways;
Her sweet communion, solemn vows,
Her hymns of love and praise.

Sure as Thy truth shall last,
To Zion shall be given,
The brightest glories earth can yield,
And bright bliss of heaven.

Timothy Dwight (1752–1817)

God's Word

I was glad when they said to me,
"Let us go into the house of the Lord."

...

For the sake of my brethren and companions,
I will now say, "Peace be within you."
Because of the house of the Lord our God
I will seek your good.
—Psalm 122:1, 8–9

And let us consider one another
in order to stir up love and good works,
not forsaking the assembling of ourselves together,
as is the manner of some,
but exhorting one another,
and so much the more as you see the Day approaching.
—Hebrews 10:24–25

Unless the Lord builds the house,
they labor in vain who build it;
unless the Lord guards the city,
the watchman stays awake in vain.
—Psalm 127:1

Reflection

I never understood why going to church made you a hypocrite,
because nobody goes to church because they are perfect.
If you've got it all together, you don't need to go to church.
You can just go jogging with all the other
perfect people on Sunday morning.
—Rich Mullins (1955–1997)

The Haven of Rest

My soul in sad exile was out on life's sea,
So burdened with sin and distress,
Till I heard a sweet voice, saying,
"Make Me your choice."
And I entered the "Haven of Rest."

I yielded myself to His tender embrace,
In faith, taking hold of the Word,
My fetters fell off
And I anchored my soul.
The "Haven of Rest" is my Lord.

The song of my soul, since the Lord made me whole
Has been the old story so blest,
Of Jesus, who will save
Whosoever will have
A home in the "Haven of Rest."

How precious the thought that we all may recline,
Like John, the beloved so blest,
On Jesus' strong arm
Where no tempest can harm,
Secure in the "Haven of Rest."

O come to the Savior, He patiently waits
To save by His power divine;
Come, anchor your soul
In the "Haven of Rest"
And say "My Beloved is mine."

I've anchored my soul
In the "Haven of Rest"
I'll sail the wide seas no more.
The tempest may sweep
Over the wild stormy deep,
In Jesus, I'm safe evermore.

Henry Lake Gilmore (1836–1920)

God's Word

I will both lie down in peace, and sleep;
for You alone, O Lord,
make me dwell in safety.
—Psalm 4:8

But from there you will seek the Lord your God,
and you will find Him, if you seek Him
with all your heart and with all your soul.
—Deuteronomy 4:29

So that they should seek the Lord,
in the hope that they might grope for Him and find Him,
though He is not far from each one of us;
for in Him we live
and move and have our being,
as also some of your own poets have said.
—Acts 17:27–28

Reflection

If you find yourself further from God
than you were yesterday,
you can be quite sure who moved.
—Unknown

Who at My Door Is Standing?

All through the dark hours dreary,
Knocking again is He.
Jesus, art Thou not weary,
Waiting so long for me?

Whispering Hope

Soft as the voice of an angel,
Breathing a lesson unheard,
Hope, with a gentle persuasion
Whispers her comforting word.

My Lord, I Did Not Choose You

Lord, 'tis not that I did choose You;
That, I know, could never be,
For this heart would still refuse You
Had your grace not chosen me.

You removed the sin that stained me,
Cleansing me to be Your own;
For this purpose You ordained me,
That I live for you alone.

It was grace in Christ that called me,
Taught my darkened heart and mind,
Else the world had yet enthralled me
To Your heavenly glories blind.

Now I worship none above You;
For Your grace alone I thirst,
Knowing well that, if I love You,
You, Father, loved me first.

Haste then on from grace to glory,
Armed by faith and winged by prayer.
All but heaven is transitory;
God's own hand shall guide us there.

Soon shall end this earthly story;
Swift shall pass the pilgrim days,
Hope soon change to heavenly glory,
Faith to sight and prayer to praise.

Josiah Conder (1789–1855)

God's Word

"You did not choose Me, but I chose you
and appointed you that you should go and bear fruit,
and that your fruit should remain,
that whatever you ask the Father in My name He may give you."
—John 15:16

But we are bound to give thanks to God always for you,
brethren beloved by the Lord,
because God from the beginning chose you
for salvation through sanctification
by the Spirit and belief in the truth,
to which He called you by our gospel,
for the obtaining of the glory of our Lord Jesus Christ.
—2 Thessalonians 2:13–14

For you *are* a holy people to the Lord your God,
and the Lord has chosen you to be a people for Himself.
—Deuteronomy 14:2

Reflection

Blessed Lord Jesus,
no human mind could conceive or invent the gospel.
Blessed be Thou, O Father, for contriving this way.
—From *The Valley of Vision: A Collection of Puritan Prayers and Devotions*[2]

---

[2] *The Valley of Vision: A Collection of Puritan Prayers and Devotions*

The Rock That Is Higher Than I

Sometimes the shadows are deep,
And rough seems the path to the goal,
And sorrows, sometimes how they sweep
Like tempests down over the soul.

Sometimes how long seems the day,
And sometimes how weary my feet.
But toiling in life's dusty way
The Rock's blessed shadow, how sweet.

Then near to the Rock let me keep
If blessings or sorrow prevail,
Or climbing the mountain way steep,
Or walking the shadowy vale.

O, then to the Rock let me fly,
To the Rock that is higher than I.
O, safe in the Rock I will bide,
In the Rock that is higher than I.

Erastus Johnson (1826–1909)

God's Word

I will love you, O Lord, my strength.
The Lord is my rock and my fortress and my deliverer;
my God, my strength, in whom I will trust;
my shield and the horn of my salvation, my stronghold.
I will call upon the Lord, who is worthy to be praised;
so shall I be saved from my enemies.
—Psalm 18:1–3

The Lord is good.
A stronghold in the day of trouble;
and He knows those who trust in Him.
—Nahum 1:7

Hear my cry, O God; attend to my prayer.
From the end of the earth I will cry to You.
When my heart is overwhelmed;
lead me to the rock that is higher than I.
—Psalm 61:1–2

Reflection

All David had was faith and a rock—
and look what he did.
—Unknown

Once It Was the Blessing

Once it was the blessing, now it is the Lord;
Once it was the feeling, now it is His Word.
Once His gift I wanted, now the Giver own;
Once I sought for healing, now Himself alone.

Once 'twas painful trying, now 'tis perfect trust;
Once a half salvation, now the uttermost.
Once 'twas ceaseless holding, now He holds me fast;
Once 'twas constant drifting, now my anchor's cast.

Once 'twas busy planning, now 'tis trustful prayer;
Once 'twas anxious caring, now He has the care.
Once 'twas what I wanted, now what Jesus says;
Once 'twas constant asking, now 'tis ceaseless praise.

Once it was my working, His it hence shall be;
Once I tried to use Him, now He uses me.
Once the power I wanted, now the Mighty One;
Once for self I labored, now for Him alone.

Once I hoped in Jesus, now I know He's mine;
Once my lamps were dying, now they brightly shine.
Once for death I waited, now His coming hail;
And my hopes are anchored safe within the veil.

Albert B. Simpson (1843–1919)

God's Word

But now, O Lord,
You are our Father;
we are the clay, and You our potter;
and all we are the work of Your hand.
—Isaiah 64:8

Nor is there salvation in any other,
for there is no other name under heaven
given among men by which we must be saved.
—Acts 4:12

Trust in the Lord, and do good;
dwell in the land, and feed on His faithfulness.
Delight yourself also in the Lord,
and He shall give you the desires of your heart.
Commit your way to the Lord,
trust also in Him,
and He shall bring it to pass.
—Psalm 37:3–5

Reflection

It is of no use to discover our own faults and infirmities
unless the discovery prompts us to amendment.
—John Quincy Adams (1767–1848)

O for a Thousand Tongues to Sing

O for a thousand tongues to sing
My great Redeemer's praise.
The glories of my God and King,
The triumphs of His grace.

My gracious Master and my God,
Assist me to proclaim,
To spread through all the earth abroad
The honors of Thy name.

Jesus, the name that charms our fears,
That bids our sorrows cease;
'Tis music in the sinner's ears,
'Tis life and health, and peace.

He breaks the power of canceled sin,
He sets the prisoner free;
His blood can make the foulest clean;
His blood availed for me.

He speaks, and listening to His voice,
New life the dead receive,
The mournful, broken hearts rejoice,
The humble poor believe.

To God all glory, praise and love
Be now and ever given
By saints below and saints above,
The church in earth and heaven.

Charles Wesley (1707–1788)

God's Word

Make a joyful shout unto the Lord,
all ye lands!
Serve the Lord with gladness;
come before His presence with singing.
Know that the Lord, He is God;
it is He who has made us,
and not we ourselves,
We are His people and the sheep of His pasture.
—Psalm 100:1–3

Praise the Lord!
Praise God in His sanctuary;
Praise Him in His mighty firmament!
Praise Him for His might acts;
Praise Him according to His excellent greatness!
Praise Him with the sound of the trumpet;
Praise Him with the lute and harp!
Praise Him with the timbral and dance;
Praise Him with stringed instruments and flutes!
Praise Him with loud cymbals;
Praise Him with clashing cymbals!
Let everything that has breath praise the Lord.
Praise the Lord!
—Psalm 150

Reflection

Be not afraid of saying too much in the praise of God;
all the danger lies in saying too little.
—Matthew Henry (1662–1714)

Count Your Blessings

When upon life's billows you are tempest tossed.
And you are discouraged, thinking all is lost.
Count your many blessings, name them one by one,
And it will surprise you what the Lord has done.

Are you ever burdened with a load of care?
Does the cross seem heavy you are called to bear?
Count your many blessings, every doubt will fly,
And you will be singing as the days go by.

When you look at others with their lands and gold,
Think that Christ has promised you His wealth untold,
Count your many blessings—money cannot buy
Your reward in heaven nor your home on high.

So, amid the conflict, whether great or small,
Do not be discouraged, God is over all.
Count your many blessings, angels will attend.
Help and comfort give you to your journey's end.

Johnson Oatman Jr. (1856–1922)

God's Word

Giving thanks always for all things
to God the Father in the name of our Lord Jesus Christ.
—Ephesians 5:20

Rejoice always,
pray without ceasing,
in everything give thanks;
for this is the will of God in Christ Jesus for you.
—1 Thessalonians 5:16

Finally, brethren, whatever things are true,
whatever things are noble,
whatever things are just,
whatever things are pure,
whatever things are lovely,
whatever things are of good report,
if there is any virtue and if there is anything praiseworthy—
meditate on these things.
—Philippians 4:8

Reflection

The secret of happiness is to count your blessings
while others are adding up their troubles.
—Sir William Penn (1644–1718)

Guide Me, O Thou Great Jehovah

Guide me, O Thou great Jehovah,
Pilgrim through this barren land;
I am weak, but Thou are mighty,
Hold me with Thy powerful hand.
Bread of Heaven,
Feed me till I want no more.

Open now the crystal fountain,
Whence the healing stream doth flow;
Let the fire and cloudy pillar
Lead me all my journey through.
Strong deliverer,
Be Thou still my Strength and Shield.

When I tread the verge of Jordan,
Bid my anxious fears subside,
Bear me through the swelling current,
Land me safe on Canaan's side.
Songs of praises,
I will ever sing to Thee.

Musing on my habitation,
Musing on my heavenly home,
Fills my soul with holy longings;
Come, my Jesus, quickly come.
Vanity is all I see;
Lord, I long to be with Thee!

William Williams (1717–1791)

God's Word

The Lord will guide you continually,
and satisfy your soul in drought,
and strengthen your bones;
you shall be like a watered garden,
and like a spring of water, whose waters do not fail.
—Isaiah 58:11

Your word is a lamp to my feet
and a light to my path.
I have sworn and confirmed
that I will keep Your righteous judgments.
I am afflicted very much;
revive me, O Lord, according to Your word.
—Psalm 119:105–107

Trust in the Lord with all your heart,
and lean not on your own understanding;
in all your ways acknowledge Him,
and He shall direct your paths.
—Proverbs 3:5–6

Reflection

Thou will keep him in perfect peace
whose mind is stayed on Thee.
—Isaiah (prophesied ca. 740–690 BC)

Who at My Door Is Standing?

Who at my door is standing,
Patiently drawing near;
Entrance within demanding,
Who's is the voice I hear?

Lonely without He is staying,
Lonely within am I.
While I am still delaying,
Will He not pass me by?

All through the dark hours dreary,
Knocking again is He.
Jesus, art Thou not weary,
Waiting so long for me?

Door of my heart, I hasten!
Thee will I open wide.
Though He rebuke and chasten,
He shall with me abide.

Sweetly the tones are falling,
"Open the door for Me.
If thou wilt heed My calling,
I will abide with thee."

Mary Bridges Canedy Slade (1826–1882)

God's Word

Behold, I stand at the door and knock.
If anyone hears My voice and opens the door,
I will come into him
and dine with him and he with Me.
—Revelation 3:20

But, beloved, do not forget this one thing,
that with the Lord one day is as a thousand years,
and a thousand years as one day.
The Lord is not slack concerning His promise,
as some count slackness,
but is longsuffering toward us,
not willing that any should perish,
but that all should come to repentance.
—2 Peter 3:8–9

If we confess our sins,
He is faithful and just to forgive us our sins,
and to cleanse us from all unrighteousness.
—1 John 1:9

Reflection

He who wept over the city
in olden times cares still,
as He looks upon the sinning
and the suffering of today.
—Amy Carmichael (1867–1951)

Take My Life and Let It Be

Take my life and let it be
Consecrated, Lord, to Thee.
Take my moments and my days;
Let them flow in ceaseless praise.

Take my hands and let them move
At the impulse of Thy love.
Take my feet and let them be
Swift and beautiful for Thee.

Take my voice and let me sing
Always, only, for my King.
Take my lips and let them be
Filled with messages from Thee.

Take my silver and my gold;
Not a mite would I withhold.
Take my intellect and use
Every power as Thou shalt choose.

Take my will and make it Thine;
It shall be no longer mine.
Take my heart, it is Thine own;
It shall be Thy royal throne.

Take my love, my Lord, I pour
At Thy feet it's treasure store.
Take myself and I will be
Ever, only all for Thee.

Francis Ridley Havergal (1836–1879)

God's Word

I beseech you therefore, brethren,
by the mercies of God,
that you present your bodies a living sacrifice,
holy, acceptable to God,
which is your reasonable service.
And do not be conformed to this world,
but be transformed by the renewing of your mind,
that you may prove what is that good
and acceptable and perfect will of God.
—Romans 12:1–2

Do not love the world or the things in the world.
If anyone loves the world,
the love of the Father is not in him.
For all that is in the world—the lust of the flesh,
the lust of the eyes, and the pride of life—
is not of the Father but is of the world.
And the world is passing away,
and the lust of it;
but he who does the will of God abides forever.
—1 John 2:15–17

Reflection

Belief is a wise wager.
If you gain, you gain all;
if you lose, you lose nothing.
Wager, then, without hesitation, that He exists!
—Blaise Pascal (1623–1662)

Whispering Hope

Soft as the voice of an angel,
Breathing a lesson unheard,
Hope, with a gentle persuasion
Whispers her comforting word.
"Wait till the darkness is over,
Wait till the tempest is done,
Hope for the sunshine tomorrow
After the shower is gone."

If, in the dusk of the twilight,
Dim be the region afar,
Will not the deepening darkness
Brighten the glimmering star?
Then, when the night is upon us,
Why should the heart sink away?
When the dark midnight is over,
Watch for the breaking of day.

Hope, as an anchor so steadfast,
Rends the dark veil for the soul,
Whither the Master has entered,
Robbing the grave of its goal.
Come then, oh, come, glad fruition,
Come to my sad, weary heart.
Come, O Thou blest hope of glory,
Never, oh, never depart.

Whispering hope,
Oh, how welcome thy voice,
Making my heart
In its sorrow, rejoice.

Septimus Winner (1827–1902)

God's Word

For we were saved in this hope,
but hope that is seen is not hope;
for why does one still hope for what he sees?
But if we hope for what we do not see,
we eagerly wait for it with perseverance.
—Romans 8:24–25

That having been justified by His grace
we should become heirs according to the hope of eternal life.
—Titus 3:7

Rejoicing in hope,
patient in tribulation,
continuing steadfastly in prayer.
—Romans 12:12

Reflection

None of us will ever accomplish anything
excellent or commanding until we listen
to the whispers which are heard by us alone.
—Thomas Carlyle (1795–1881)

We'll Understand It Better By and By

We are often tossed and driven
On the restless sea of time,
Somber skies and howling tempests
Oft succeed a bright sunshine;
In that land of perfect day,
When the mists are rolled away,
We will understand it better by and by.

We are often destitute
Of the things that life demands,
Want of food and want of shelter,
Thirsty hills and barren lands;
But we're trusting in the Lord,
And according to His word,
We will understand it better by and by.

Trials dark on every hand,
And we cannot understand
All the ways that God would lead us
To that blessed promised land;
But He guides us with His eye,
And we'll follow till we die,
For we'll understand it better by and by.

Temptation, hidden snares
Often take us unawares,
And our hearts are made to bleed
For a thoughtless word or deed;
And we wonder why the test
When we try to do our best,
But we'll understand it better by and by.

By and by, when the morning comes,
When the saints of God are gathered home;
We will tell the story how we've overcome,
And we'll understand it better by and by.

Charles Albert Tindley (1851–1933)

God's Word

Trust in the Lord with all your heart,
and lean not on your own understanding;
in all your ways acknowledge Him,
and He shall direct your paths.
—Proverbs 3:5–6

He has shown you, O man, what is good;
and what does the Lord require of you
but to do justly, to love mercy,
and to walk humbly with your God?
—Micah 6:8

Being confident of this very thing,
that He who has begun a good work in you
will complete it until the day of Jesus Christ.
—Philippians 1:6

Reflection

Charles Tindley, the son of a slave, would become a master of theology
and music. He wrote the enduring words of "We'll Understand It Better
By and By" following the sudden death of his beloved wife, Daisy.

Softly and Tenderly, Jesus Is Calling

Come home, come home,
You who are weary, come home.
Earnestly, tenderly, Jesus is calling.
Calling, O sinner, come home.

Trusting Jesus, That Is All

Even when my faith is small,
Trusting Jesus, that is all.

Thou Thinkest, Lord, of Me

Amid the trials which I meet,
Amid the thorns that pierce my feet,
One thought remains supremely sweet,
Thou thinkest, Lord, of me.

The cares of life come thronging fast,
Upon my soul their shadows cast;
Their gloom reminds my heart at last,
Thou thinkest, Lord, of me.

Let shadows come, let shadows go,
Let life be bright or dark with woe,
I am content, for this I know.
Thou thinkest, Lord, of me.

Thou thinkest, Lord, of me,
What need I fear,
Since Thou art near,
Thou thinkest, Lord, of me.

Edmond S. Lorenz (1854–1942)

God's Word

For I know the thoughts that I think
toward you, says the Lord,
thoughts of peace and not of evil,
to give you a future and a hope.
Then you will call upon Me
and go and pray to Me,
And I will listen to you.
And you will seek Me and find Me,
When you search for Me with all your heart.
—Jeremiah 29:11–13

Therefore humble yourselves
under the mighty hand of God,
that He may exalt you in due time,
casting all your care upon Him,
for He cares for you.
—1 Peter 5:6

Just as He chose us in Him
before the foundation of the world,
that we should be holy
and without blame before Him in love.
—Ephesians 1:4

Reflection

God loves each of us
as if there were only one of us.
—Saint Augustine (354–430)

Trusting Jesus, That Is All

Simply trusting every day,
Trusting through a stormy way;
Even when my faith is small,
Trusting Jesus, that is all.

Brightly does His spirit shine,
Into this poor heart of mine;
While He leads I cannot fall;
Trusting Jesus, that is all.

Singing if my way is clear,
Praying if the path be drear;
If in danger, on Him I call,
Trusting Jesus, that is all.

Trusting Him while life shall last,
Trusting Him till earth be past;
Till within the jasper walls,
Trusting Jesus, that is all.

Trusting as the moments fly,
Trusting as the days go by;
Trusting Him whatever befall,
Trusting Jesus, that is all.

Edgar P. Stites (1836–1921)

God's Word

For I consider that the sufferings of this present time
are not worthy to be compared
with the glory which shall be revealed in us.
For the earnest expectation of the creation
eagerly waits for the revealing of the sons of God.
—Romans 8:18–19

Jesus said to him,
"I am the way,
the truth, and the life.
No one comes to the Father
except through Me."
—John 14:6

And now, O Lord God, You are God,
And Your words are true,
and You have promised this goodness to your servant.
—2 Samuel 7:28

Reflection

Dear God,
I do not know You, God,
because I am in the way.
Please help me to push myself aside.
—*A Prayer Journal*,[3] Flannery O'Connor (1925–1964)

---

[3] Flannery O'Connor, *A Prayer Journal*.

The Ninety and Nine

There were ninety and nine that safely lay
In the shelter of the fold,
But one was out on the hills away,
Far off from the gates of gold.
Away on the mountains wild and bare,
Away from the tender Shepherd's care.

"Lord, Thou hast here Thy ninety and nine;
Are they not enough for Thee?"
But the Shepherd made answer, "This of Mine
Has wondered away from Me.
And although the road be rough and steep.
I go to the desert to find My sheep."

But none of the ransomed ever knew
How deep were the waters crossed;
Nor how dark was the night the Lord passed through
Ere He found His sheep that was lost.
Out in the desert He heard its cry,
Sick and helpless and ready to die.

"Lord, whence are those blood drops all the way,
That mark out the mountain's track?"
"They were shed for one who had gone astray
Ere the Shepherd could bring him back,"
"Lord, whence are Thy hands so rent and torn?"
"They are pierced tonight by many a thorn."

And all through the mountains, thunder-riven,
And up from the rocky steep,
There arose a glad cry to the gate of heaven,
"Rejoice! I have found My sheep!"
And the angels echoed around the throne,
"Rejoice, for the Lord brings back His own!"

Elizabeth C. Clephane (1830–1869)

God's Word

"What do you think?
If a man has a hundred sheep,
and one of them goes astray,
does he not leave the ninety-nine
and go to the mountains to seek the one that is straying?
And if he should find it, assuredly, I say to you,
he rejoices more over that sheep
than over the ninety-nine that did not go astray."
—Matthew 18:12–13

For you were like sheep going astray,
but have now returned to the
Shepherd and Overseer of your souls.
—1 Peter 2:25

I have gone astray like a lost sheep;
seek Your servant,
for I do not forget Your commandments.
—Psalm 119:176

Reflection

I once was lost but now am found,
was blind but now I see.
—John Newton (1725–1807)

My Hope Is Built on Nothing Less

My hope is built on nothing less
Than Jesus' blood and righteousness.
I dare not trust the sweetest frame,
But wholly lean on Jesus' name.

When darkness seems to hide His face,
I rest on His unchanging grace.
In every high and stormy gale,
My anchor holds within the veil.

His oath, His covenant, His blood,
Support me in the whelming flood.
When all around my soul gives way,
He then is all my Hope and Stay.

When He shall come with trumpet sound,
Oh, may I then in Him be found;
Clothed in His righteousness alone,
Faultless to stand before the Throne!

On Christ, the Solid Rock I stand;
All other ground is sinking sand.

Edward Mote (1797–1874)

God's Word

"Therefore whoever hears these sayings of Mine,
and does them,
I will liken him to a wise man
who built his house on the rock:
and the rain descended,
the floods came, and the winds blew
and beat on that house; and it did not fall,
for it was founded on the rock.
But everyone who hears these sayings of Mine,
and does not do them,
will be like a foolish man
who built his house on the sand:
and the rain descended,
the floods came, and the winds blew
and beat on that house; and it fell.
And great was its fall."
—Matthew 7:24–27

For I proclaim the name of the Lord:
ascribe greatness to our God.
He is the Rock, His work is perfect;
for all His ways are justice,
a God of truth and without injustice;
righteous and upright is He.
—Deuteronomy 32:3–4

Reflection

Aim at heaven and you will get earth thrown in.
Aim at earth and you get neither.
—C. S. Lewis (1898–1963)

Softly and Tenderly, Jesus Is Calling

Softly and tenderly, Jesus is calling,
Calling for you and for me.
See, on the portals, He's waiting and watching,
Watching for you and for me.

Why should we tarry when Jesus is pleading,
Pleading for you and for me?
Why should we linger and heed not His mercies,
Mercies for you and for me?

Time is now fleeting, the moments are passing,
Passing from you and from me;
Shadows are gathering, deathbeds are coming,
Coming for you and for me.

O, for the wonderful love He has promised,
Promised for you and for me.
Though we have sinned, He has mercy and pardon,
Pardon for you and for me.

Come home, come home,
You who are weary, come home.
Earnestly, tenderly, Jesus is calling.
Calling, O sinner, come home.

Will Lamartine Thompson (1847–1909)

God's Word

"In My Father's house are many mansions;
if it were not so, I would have told you.
I go to prepare a place for you.
And if I go and prepare a place for you,
I will come again and receive you to Myself;
that where I am, there you may be also.
And where I go you know,
and the way you know."
—John 14:2–4

For our citizenship is in heaven,
from which we also eagerly wait for the Savior,
The Lord Jesus Christ,
who will transform our lowly body
that it may be conformed to His glorious body,
according to the working by which
He is able even to subdue all things to Himself.
—Philippians 3:20–21

Reflection

I am still in the land of the dying;
I shall soon be in the land of the living.
—Dying words of John Newton (1725–1807)

Come, Ye Disconsolate

Come, ye disconsolate,
Wherever ye languish.
Come to the mercy seat,
Fervently kneel.

Here bring your wounded hearts,
Here tell your anguish;
Earth has no sorrow
That heaven cannot heal.

Joy of the desolate,
Light of the straying,
Hope of the penitent,
Fadeless and pure.

Here speaks the Comforter,
In mercy saying,
"Earth has no sorrow
That heaven cannot cure."

Here see the Bread of life,
See waters flowing
Forth from the throne of God,
Pure from above.

Come to the feast of love,
Come, ever knowing
Earth has no sorrow
But heaven can remove.

Thomas Moore (1779–1852)
Later edited and added to by Thomas Hastings (1784–1872)

God's Word

For in You, O Lord, I hope;
You will hear, O Lord, my God.
For I said, "Hear me, lest they rejoice over me,
lest, when my foot slips,
they exalt themselves against me."
For I am ready to fall,
and my sorrow is continually before me.
For I will declare my iniquity;
I will be in anguish over my sin.
But my enemies are vigorous,
and they are strong;
and those who hate me wrongfully have multiplied.
Those also who render evil for good,
they are my adversaries,
because I follow what is good.
Do not forsake me, O Lord;
O my God, be not far from me!
Make haste to help me,
O Lord, my salvation!
—Psalm 38:15–22

Reflection

As long as there is one upright man,
as long as there is one compassionate woman,
that very contagion may spread, and desolation disappear.
Hope is the thing that is left us in a bad time.
—E. B. White (1899–1985)

Savior, Like a Shepherd Lead Us

Savior, like a shepherd, lead us,
Much we need Thy tender care;
In Thy pleasant pastures, feed us,
For our use Thy folds prepare.

We are Thine, Thou dost befriend us,
Be the guardian of our way;
Keep Thy flock from sin, defend us,
Seek us when we go astray.

Thou hast promised to receive us,
Poor and sinful though we be;
Thou hast mercy to relieve us,
Grace to cleanse and power to free.

Early let us seek Thy favor;
Early let us do Thy will;
Blessed Lord and only Savior.
With Thy love our bosoms fill.

Dorothy A. Thrupp (1779–1847)

God's Word

Give ear, O Shepherd of Israel,
You who lead Joseph like a flock;
You who dwell between the cherubim, shine forth!
Before Ephraim, Benjamin, and Manasseh,
Stir up Your strength,
and come and save us!
Restore us, O God;
cause Your face to shine,
and we shall be saved!
—Psalm 80:1–3

"And do not seek what you should eat
or what you should drink, nor have an anxious mind.
For all these things the nations of the world seek after,
and you Father knows that you need these things.
But seek the kingdom of God,
and all these things shall be added to you.
Do not fear, little flock,
for it is your Father's good pleasure
to give you the kingdom."
—Luke 12:29–32

Reflection

I am like the sick sheep that strays from the rest of the flock.
Unless the Good Shepherd takes me on His shoulders
and carries me back to His fold,
my steps will falter and my feet will give way.
—Saint Jerome (342–420)

Near to the Heart of God

There is a place of quiet rest,
Near to the heart of God.
A place where sin cannot molest,
Near to the heart of God.

There is a place of comfort sweet,
Near to the heart of God.
A place where we our Savior meet,
Near to the heart of God.

There is a place of full release,
Near to the heart of God.
A place where all is joy and peace,
Near to the heart of God.

O Jesus, blessed Redeemer,
Sent from the heart of God;
Hold us who wait before Thee,
Near to the heart of God.

Cleland B. McAfee (1866–1944)

God's Word

Therefore, having been justified by faith,
we have peace with God
through our Lord Jesus Christ,
through whom also we have access by faith
into this grace in which we stand,
and rejoice in hope of the glory of God.
And not only that, but we also glory in tribulations,
knowing that tribulation produces perseverance;
and perseverance, character;
and character, hope.
Now hope does not disappoint,
because the love of God
has been poured out in our hearts
by the Holy Spirit who was given to us.
—Romans 5:1–5

But God, who is rich in mercy,
because of His great love with which He loved us,
even when we were dead in trespasses,
made us alive together with Christ
(by grace you have been saved),
and raised us up together, and made us sit together
in the heavenly places in Christ Jesus.
—Ephesians 2:4–6

Reflection

It will greatly comfort you
if you can see God's hand
in both your losses and your crosses.
—Charles Spurgeon (1832–1892)

Breathe on Me, Breath of God

Breathe on me, breath of God,
Fill me with life anew,
That I may love what Thou dost love,
And do what Thou wouldst do.

Breathe on me, breath of God,
Until my heart is pure,
Until my will is one with yours,
To do and to endure.

Breathe on me, breath of God,
Until I am wholly Thine,
Until this earthly part of me,
Glows with Thy fire divine.

Breathe on me, breath of God,
So shall I never die,
But live with you the perfect life
Of Thine eternity.

Edwin Hatch (1835–1889)

God's Word

And the Lord God formed man
of the dust of the ground,
and breathed into his nostrils the breath of life;
and man became a living being.
—Genesis 2:7

The Spirit of God has made me,
and the breath of the Almighty gives me life.
—Job 33:4

Also He said to me, "Prophesy to the breath,
prophesy, son of man, and say to the breath,
'Thus says the Lord God:
"Come from the four winds, O breath,
and breathe on the slain, that they may live."'"
So I prophesied as He commanded me,
and breath came into them,
and they lived, and stood upon their feet,
an exceedingly great army.
—Ezekiel 37:9–10

Reflection

The best things in life are nearest:
breath in your nostrils,
light in your eyes, flowers at your feet, duties at your hand,
the path of right just before you.
Then do not grasp at the stars but do life's plain,
common work as it comes,
certain that daily duties and daily bread are the sweetest things in life.
—Robert Louis Stevenson (1850–1894)

Brethren, We Have Met to Worship

Brethren, we have met to worship and adore the Lord our God.
Will you pray with all your power while we try to preach the word?
All is vain unless the Spirit of the Holy One comes down;
Brethren, pray, and holy manna will be showered all around.

Brethren, see poor sinners round you, trembling on the brink of woe;
Death is coming, hell is moving; can you bear to let them go?
See our fathers, see our mothers, and our children sinking down?
Brethren, pray, and holy manna will be showered all around.

Sister, will you join and help us? Moses' sisters aided him;
Will you help the trembling mourners who
are struggling hard with sin?
Tell them all about the Savior, tell them that He will be found;
Sisters, pray, and holy manna will be showered all around.

Is there here a trembling jailer, seeking grace and filled with fears?
Is there here a weeping Mary, pouring forth a flood of tears?
Brethren, join your cries to help them; sisters, let your prayers abound.
Pray! O pray, that holy manna may be scattered all around.

Let us love our God supremely, let us love each other too;
Let us love and pray for sinners, till our God makes all things new.
Then He'll call us home to heaven, at His table we'll sit down.
Christ will gird Himself and serve us, with sweet manna all around.

George Atkins (1793–1827)

God's Word

And they continued steadfastly in the apostles' doctrine
and fellowship, in the breaking of bread, and in prayers.
Then fear came upon every soul,
and many wonders and signs were done through the apostles.
Now all who believed were together,
and had all things in common.
—Acts 2:42–44

Let us hold fast the confession
of our hope without wavering,
for He who promised is faithful.
And let us consider one another
in order to stir up love and good works,
not forsaking the assembling of ourselves together.
—Hebrews 10:23–25

Reflection

Take heed, then, often to come together
to give thanks to God and show forth His praise.
For when you assemble frequently in the same place,
the powers of Satan are destroyed,
and the destruction at which he aims is
prevented by the unity of your faith.
—Saint Ignatius of Antioch (d. 108)

Come, Thou Fount of Every Blessing

Prone to wander, Lord, I feel it,
Prone to leave the God I love.
Here's my heart, O take and seal it,
Seal it for Thy courts above.

Just a Closer Walk with Thee

Through this world of toil and snares,
If I falter, Lord, who cares?
Who with me my burden shares?
None but Thee, dear Lord, none but Thee.

Come, Thou Fount of Every Blessing

Come, Thou fount of every blessing,
Tune my heart to sing Thy grace;
Streams of mercy, never ceasing
Call for songs of loudest praise.

Teach me some melodious sonnet
Sung by flaming tongues above;
Praise the mount! I'm fixed upon it,
Mount of Thy redeeming love.

Here I raise my Ebenezer,
Hither by Thy help I've come;
And I hope, by Thy good pleasure,
Safely to arrive at home.

Jesus sought me when a stranger,
Wandering from the face of God;
He, to save my soul from danger,
Interposed His precious blood.

Oh, to grace how great a debtor
Daily I'm constrained to be!
Let Thy goodness like a fetter,
Bind my wandering heart to Thee.

Prone to wander, Lord, I feel it,
Prone to leave the God I love;
Here's my heart, O take and seal it,
Seal it for Thy courts above.

Robert Robinson* (1735–1790)

* Robinson wrote this poem at the age of twenty-two.

God's Word

O Lord God of hosts, hear my prayer;
give ear, O God of Jacob!
O God, behold our shield,
and look upon the face of Your anointed.
For a day in Your courts is better than a thousand.
I would rather be a doorkeeper
in the house of my God
than dwell in the tents of wickedness.
For the Lord God is a sun and shield;
the Lord will give grace and glory;
no good thing will He withhold
from those who walk uprightly.
O Lord of hosts,
blessed is the man who trusts in You!
—Psalm 84:8–12

For if we live, we live to the Lord;
and if we die, we die to the Lord.
Therefore, whether we live or die, we are the Lord's.
—Romans 14:8

Reflection

Count not of great importance
who is for you, or against you,
but let this be your aim and care,
that God be with you in everything you do.
Have a good conscience,
and God shall defend you.
—Thomas à Kempis (1380–1471)

Beautiful Isle of Somewhere

Somewhere the sun is shining,
Somewhere the songbirds swell;
Hush, then, thy sad repining,
God lives, and all is well.

Somewhere the day is longer,
Somewhere the task is done;
Somewhere the heart is stronger,
Somewhere the prize is won.

Somewhere the load is lifted,
Close by an open gate;
Somewhere the clouds are rifted,
Somewhere the angels wait.

Somewhere, somewhere,
Beautiful Isle of Somewhere;
Land of the true, where we live anew,
Beautiful Isle of Somewhere.

Jessie Hunter Brown Pounds (1861–1921)

God's Word

Now I saw a new heaven and a new earth,
for the first heaven and the first earth had passed away.

…

… God Himself will be with them
and be their God.
And God will wipe away every tear from their eyes;
there shall be no more death,
nor sorrow, nor crying.
there shall be no more pain,
for the former things have passed away.
Then He who sat on the throne said,
"Behold, I make all things new."
—Revelation 21:1, 3–5

He will swallow up death forever,
and the Lord God will wipe away tears from all faces;
the rebuke of His people
He will take away from all the earth;
for the Lord has spoken.
—Isaiah 25:8

Reflection

Never fear dying, beloved.
Dying is the last, but the least matter
that a Christian has to be anxious about.
Fear living—that is the hard battle to fight,
a stern discipline to endure, a rough voyage to undergo.
—Charles Spurgeon (1834–1892)

Love Lifted Me

I was sinking deep in sin,
Far from the peaceful shore;
Very deeply stained within,
Sinking to rise no more.
But the Master of the sea,
Heard my despairing cry,
From the waters lifted me,
Now safe am I.

All my heart to Him I give,
Ever to Him I'll cling;
In His blessed presence live,
Ever His praises sing.
Love so mighty and so true,
Merits my soul's best songs;
Faithful, loving service, too,
To Him belong.

Souls in danger, look above;
Jesus completely saves.
He will lift you by His love
Out of the angry waves.
He's the Master of seas,
Billows His will obey;
He your Savior wants to be—
Be saved today!

Love lifted me,
When nothing else could help,
Love lifted me.

James Rowe (1865–1933)

God's Word

Beloved, let us love one another,
for love is of God; and everyone who loves
is born of God and knows God.
He who does not love
does not know God, for God is love.
In this the love of God was manifested toward us,
that God has sent His only begotten Son into the world,
that we might live through Him.
In this is love, not that we loved God,
but that He loved us
and sent His Son
to be the propitiation for our sins.
—1 John 4:7–10

I waited patiently for the Lord;
and He inclined to me,
and heard my cry.
He also brought me up out of a horrible pit,
out of the miry clay,
and set my feet upon a rock,
and established my steps.
He has put a new song in my mouth—
praise to our God.
—Psalm 40:1–3

Reflection

If we do not know ourselves to be full of pride,
ambition, lust, weakness, misery and injustice,
we are indeed blind.
And if, knowing this, we do not desire deliverance,
what can we say of a man?
—Blaise Pascal (1623–1662)

Immortal, Invisible, God Only Wise

Immortal, invisible,
God only wise;
In light inaccessible, hid from our eyes.
Most blessed, most glorious, the Ancient of Days,
Almighty, victorious, Thy great name we praise.

Unresting, unhasting,
And silent as light;
Nor wanting, nor wasting, Thou rulest in might.
Thy justice, like mountains, high soaring above,
Thy clouds, which are fountains of goodness and love.

To all, life He giveth,
To both great and small;
In all life Thou livest, the true life of all,
We blossom and flourish as leaves on the tree,
And wither and perish—but naught changeth Thee.

Great Father of glory,
Pure Father of light,
Thine angels adore Thee, all veiling their sight;
All laud we would render, O help us to see,
'Tis only the splendor of light hideth Thee.

Walter Chalmers Smith (1824–1908)

God's Word

Now to the King eternal,
immortal, invisible,
to God who alone is wise,
be honor and glory forever and ever.
Amen.
—1 Timothy 1:17

With Him are wisdom and strength,
He has counsel and understanding.
If He breaks a thing down, it cannot be rebuilt;
if He imprisons a man, there can be no release.
If He withhold the waters, they dry up;
if He sends them out, they overwhelm the earth.
With Him are strength and prudence.
The deceived and the deceiver are His.
—Job 12:13–16

Reflection

Oh, Thou who art!
Ecclesiastes names Thee the Almighty.
Maccabees names Thee Creator;
the epistle to the Ephesians names Thee Liberty …
the Psalms name Thee Wisdom and Truth;
John names Thee Light;
the book of Kings names Thee Lord;
Exodus calls Thee Providence;
Leviticus, Holiness; Esdras, Justice;
Creation calls Thee God;
Man names Thee Father;
but Solomon names Thee Compassion,
and that is the most beautiful of all Thy names.
—Victor Hugo (1802–1885)

O Master, Let Me Walk with Thee

O Master let me walk with Thee,
In lowly paths of service free;
Tell me Thy secret, help me bear
The strain of toil, the fret of care.

Help me the slow of heart to move
By some clear, winning word of love.
Teach me the wayward feet to stay,
And guide them in the homeward way.

O Master let me walk with Thee,
Before the taunting Pharisee;
Help me to bear the sting of spite,
The hate of men who hide Thy light.

Teach me Thy patience; still with Thee
In closer, dearer, company;
In work that keeps faith sweet and strong,
In trust that triumphs over wrong.

In hope that sends a shining ray
Far down the future's broadening way,
In peace that only Thou can give,
With Thee, O Master, let me live.

Washington Gladden (1836–1918)

God's Word

I will walk among you and be your God,
and you shall be My people.
—Leviticus 26:12

Therefore you shall keep the commandments
of the Lord your God,
to walk in His ways and to fear Him.
—Deuteronomy 8:6

For we are His workmanship,
created in Christ Jesus for good works,
which God prepared beforehand that we should walk in them.
—Ephesians 2:10

Noah was a just man, perfect in his generations.
Noah walked with God.
—Genesis 6:9

Reflection

The most important thought that ever occupied my
mind is that of my individual responsibility to God.
—Daniel Webster (1782–1852)

Where We'll Never Grow Old

I have heard of a land
On a faraway strand,
'Tis the beautiful home of the soul;
Built by Jesus on high,
Where we never shall die,
In a land where we never grow old.

In the beautiful home
Where we'll never more roam
We shall be in the sweet by and by;
Happy praise to the King
Through eternity sing,
In a land where we never shall die.

When our work here is done
And the life crown is won,
And our troubles and trials are o'er;
All our sorrow will end,
And our voices will blend,
With the loved ones who've gone on before.

James C. Moore (1888–1962)

God's Word

Brethren, I do not count myself to have apprehended;
but one thing I do, forgetting those things
which are behind and reaching forward
to those things which are ahead,
I press toward the goal for the prize
of the upward call of God in Christ Jesus.

...

For our citizenship is in heaven,
from which we also eagerly wait
for the Savior, the Lord Jesus Christ,
who will transform our lowly body
that it may be conformed to His glorious body,
according to the working by which
He is able even to subdue all things to Himself.
—Philippians 3:13–14, 20–21

My flesh and my heart fail;
but God is the strength of my heart
and my portion forever.
—Psalm 73:26

Reflection

Grow old along with me!
The best is yet to be,
the last of life, for which the first was made.
Our times are in His hand who said,
"A whole I planned, youth shows but half;
trust God: See all, nor be afraid!"
—Robert Browning (1812–1889)

Jesus! What a Friend for Sinners

Jesus! What a friend for sinners!
Jesus! Lover of my soul;
Friends may fail me, foes assail me,
He, my Savior, makes me whole.

Jesus! What a strength in weakness!
Let me hide myself in Him;
Tempted, tried and sometimes failing,
He, my strength, my victory wins.

Jesus! What a help in sorrow!
While the billows over me roll;
Even when my heart is breaking,
He, my comfort, helps my soul.

Jesus! I do now receive Him,
More than all in Him I find;
He hath granted me forgiveness,
I am His, and He is mine.

Hallelujah! What a Savior!
Hallelujah! What a friend!
Saving, helping, keeping, loving,
He is with me to the end.

J. Wilbur Chapman
(1859–1918)

God's Word

"As the Father loved Me, I also have loved you;
abide in My love."
—John 15:9

But God demonstrates His own love toward us,
in that while we were still sinners,
Christ died for us.
—Romans 5:8

Behold what manner of love the Father has bestowed on us,
that we should be called children of God!
—1 John 3:1

Therefore be imitators of God as dear children.
And walk in love, as Christ also has loved us
and given Himself for us,
an offering and a sacrifice to God
for a sweet-smelling aroma.
—Ephesians 5:1–2

Reflection

I strive to remember two things:
that I am a great sinner
and that Christ is a great Savior.
—John Newton (1725–1807)

Faith of Our Fathers

Faith of our fathers, living still,
In spite of dungeon, fire and sword;
Oh, how our hearts beat high with joy
Whenever we hear that glorious Word!

Faith of our fathers, we will strive
To win all nations unto Thee;
And through the truth that comes from God,
We all shall then be truly free.

Faith of our fathers, we will love
Both friend and foe in all our strife,
And preach Thee, too, as love knows how
By kindly words and virtuous life.

Faith of our fathers,
Holy faith!
We will be true
To Thee till death.

Frederick William Faber (1814–1863)

God's Word

By faith, Abel offered to God a more excellent sacrifice ...
By faith, Enoch was taken away so that he did not see death ...
By faith, Noah ... prepared an ark ...
By faith, Abraham obeyed ...
By faith, Sarah herself received strength to conceive ...
By faith, Abraham offered up Isaac ...
By faith, Isaac blessed Jacob and Esau ...
By faith, Jacob blessed the sons of Joseph ...
By faith, Joseph, when he was dying ... gave instructions ...
By faith, Moses ... forsook Egypt ... and passed through the Red Sea ...
By faith, the walls of Jericho fell down ...
By faith, the harlot, Rahab did not perish ...
And what more can I say? For the time would fail me
to tell of Gideon, Barak, Samson, Jephthah, David, Samuel
and the prophets.
Others were tortured, not accepting deliverance,
that they might obtain a better resurrection.
Still others had trial of mockings and scourgings,
yes, and of chains and imprisonment.
They were stoned, they were sawn in two,
were tempted, were slain with the sword.

And all these, having obtained a good testimony through faith,
did not receive the promise.
—Taken from Hebrews 11, often called the "Faith Hall of Fame"

Reflection

The general principles on which the fathers
achieved independence
were the general principles of Christianity.
I will avow that I then believed, and now believe,
that those general principles of Christianity
are as eternal and immutable
as the existence and attributes of God.
—John Adams (1735–1826)

150

Leave It There

If the world from you withholds
Of its silver and its gold,
And you have to get along with meager fare,
Just remember in His word,
How He feeds the little bird—
Take your burden to the Lord
And leave it there.

If your body suffers pain
And your health you can't regain,
And your soul is slowly sinking in despair,
Jesus knows the pain you feel,
He can save and He can heal—
Take your burden to the Lord
And leave it there.

When your enemies assail
And your heart begins to fail,
Don't forget that God in heaven answers prayer;
He will make a way for you
And will lead you safely through—
Take your burden to the Lord
And leave it there.

When your youthful days are gone
And old age is stealing on,
And your body bends beneath the weight of care;
He will never leave you then,
He'll go with you to the end—
Take your burden to the Lord
And leave it there.

Leave it there, leave it there,
Take your burden to the Lord and leave it there.
If you trust and never doubt
He will surely bring you out—
Take your burden to the Lord
And leave it there.

Charles Albert Tindley (1851–1933)

God's Word

"Most assuredly, I say to you, he who believes in Me,
the works that I do he will do also;
and greater works than these he will do, because I go to My Father.
And whatever you ask in My name, that I will do,
that the Father may be glorified in the Son.
If you ask anything in My name, I will do it."
—John 14:12–13

Hear my prayer, O Lord,
and let my cry come to You.
Do not hide Your face from me in the day of my trouble;
incline Your ear to me;
in the day that I call, answer me speedily.
—Psalm 102:1–2

The Lord is good to those who wait for Him,
to the soul who seeks Him.
—Lamentations 3:25

Reflection

All our perils are nothing
as long as we have God.
—Charles Spurgeon (1834–1892)

Just a Closer Walk with Thee

I am weak, but Thou art strong,
Jesus, keep me from all wrong.
I'll be satisfied as long
As I walk, let me walk close to Thee.

Through this world of toil and snares,
If I falter, Lord, who cares?
Who with me my burden shares?
None but Thee, dear Lord, none but Thee.

When my feeble life is o'er,
Time for me will be no more.
Guide me gently, safely o'er,
To Thy kingdom's shore, To Thy shore.

Just a closer walk with Thee,
Grant it, Jesus, is my plea.
Daily walking close to Thee,
Let it be, dear Lord, let it be.

Author unknown
(Hymns with similar lyrics appeared in the 1800s, including
"Closer Walk with Thee" by Fanny Crosby)

God's Word

But we have this treasure in earthen vessels,
that the excellence of the power may be of God and not of us.
We are hard-pressed on every side, yet not crushed;
we are perplexed, but not in despair,
persecuted, but not forsaken;
struck down, but not destroyed.
—2 Corinthians 4:7–9

Create in me a clean heart, O God,
and renew a steadfast spirit within me.
Do not cast me away from Your presence,
and do not take Your Holy Spirit from me.
—Psalm 51:10–11

Woe to those who are wise in their own eyes,
and prudent in their own sight!
—Isaiah 5:21

Reflection

Bestow on me, O Lord my God,
understanding to know You,
diligence to seek You,
and faithfulness that may finally embrace You,
through Jesus Christ our Lord.
—Thomas Aquinas (1225–1274)

Pass Me Not, O Gentle Savior

Pass me not, o gentle Savior,
Hear my humble cry.
While on others Thou art calling,
Do not pass me by.

Farther Along

Cheer up, my brother, live in the sunshine,
We'll understand it all by and by.

To God Be the Glory

To God be the glory,
Great things He hath done;
So loved He the world that He gave us His Son,
Who yielded His life an atonement for sin,
And opened the life gate that all may go in.

O perfect redemption,
The purchase of blood,
To every believer, the promise of God;
The vilest offender who truly believes,
That moment from Jesus a pardon receives.

Great things He hath taught us,
Great things He hath done.
And great our rejoicing through Jesus, the Son;
But purer and higher and greater will be,
Our wonder, our transport when Jesus we see.

Praise the Lord!
Let the earth hear His voice!
Let the people rejoice!
O come to the Father, through Jesus, the Son,
And give Him the glory,
Great things He hath done.

Fanny Jane Crosby (1820–1915)

God's Word

O Lord, our Lord,
how excellent is Your name in all the earth,
who have set Your glory above the heavens!

...

When I consider Your heavens, the work of Your fingers,
the moon and the stars, which You have ordained,
what is man that You are mindful of him,
and the son of man that You visit him?
—Psalm 8:1, 3–4

I will praise You, O Lord,
with my whole heart;
I will tell of all Your marvelous works.
I will be glad and rejoice in You;
I will sing praise to Your name, O Most High.
—Psalm 9:1–2

Let everything that has breath praise the Lord.
Praise the Lord!
—Psalm 150:6

Reflection

A man can no more diminish God's glory
by refusing to worship Him
than a lunatic can put out the sun
by scribbling the word *darkness* on the walls of his cell.
—C. S. Lewis (1898–1963)

How Beautiful Heaven Must Be

We read of a place that's called heaven,
It's made for the pure and the free;
These truths in Gods' Word He has given,
How beautiful heaven must be.

In heaven no drooping nor pining,
No wishing for elsewhere to be;
God's light is forever there shining,
How beautiful heaven must be.

Pure waters of life there are flowing,
And all who will drink may be free;
Rare jewels of splendor are glowing,
How beautiful heaven must be.

The angels so sweetly are singing,
Up there by the beautiful sea;
Sweet chords from their gold harps are ringing,
How beautiful heaven must be.

How beautiful heaven must be,
Sweet home of the happy and free;
Fair haven of rest for the weary,
How beautiful heaven must be.

Mrs. A. S. (Cordie) Bridgewater (1873–1957)

God's Word

There shall be no night there:
They need no lamp nor light of the sun,
for the Lord God gives them light.
And they shall reign forever and ever.
—Revelation 22:5

Then he said to Jesus, "Lord, remember me
when You come into Your kingdom."
And Jesus said to him, "Assuredly, I say to you,
today you will be with Me in Paradise."
—Luke 23:42–43

But as it is written:
"Eye has not seen, not ear heard,
nor have entered into the heart of man
the things which God has prepared
for those who love Him."
—1 Corinthians 2:9

Reflections

Let us not be afraid to meditate
often on the subject of heaven,
and to rejoice in the prospect of good things to come. ...
Let us take comfort
in the remembrance of the other side.
—J. C. Ryle (1816–1900)

Close to Thee

Thou my everlasting portion,
More than friend or life to me;
All along my pilgrim journey,
Savior, let me walk with Thee.

Not for ease or worldly pleasure,
Nor for fame my prayer shall be;
Gladly will I toil and suffer,
Only let me walk with Thee.

Lead me through the vale of shadows,
Bear me o'er life's fitful sea;
Then the gate of life eternal
May I enter, Lord, with Thee.

Fanny Jane Crosby (1820–1915)

God's Word

Though I walk in the midst of trouble,
You will revive me;
You will stretch out Your hand
against the wrath of my enemies,
and Your right hand will save me.
The Lord will perfect that which concerns me;
Your mercy, O Lord, endures forever;
do not forsake the works of Your hands.
—Psalm 138:7–8

Seek the Lord while He may be found,
call upon Him while He is near.
Let the wicked forsake his way,
and the unrighteous man his thoughts;
let him return to the Lord,
and He will have mercy on him;
and to our God,
for He will abundantly pardon.
—Isaiah 55:6–7

Reflection

May I always hear that you are following the guidance
of that blessed Holy Spirit that will lead you into all truth,
leaning on that Almighty Arm
that has been extended to deliver you,
trusting only in the only Savior,
and going on in your way to Him rejoicing.
—Francis Scott Key (1779–1843)

Before the Throne of God Above

Before the throne of God above,
I have a strong and perfect plea;
A great High Priest whose name is Love
Who ever lives and pleas for me.

My name is graven on His hands,
My name is written on His heart;
I know that while in heaven He stands,
No tongue can bid me thence depart.

When Satan tempts me to despair
And tells me of the guilt within,
Upward I look and see Him there
Who made an end of all my sin.

Because the sinless Savior died,
My sinful soul is counted free;
For God, the Just, is satisfied
To look on Him and pardon me.

Behold Him there, the risen Lamb,
My perfect spotless righteousness;
The great unchangeable I Am,
The King of glory and of grace.

One in Himself I cannot die,
My soul is purchased by His blood;
My life is hid with Christ on high,
With Christ, my Savior and my God.

Charitie Lees Bancroft (1841–1923)

God's Word

Seeing then that we have a great High Priest
who has passed through the heavens, Jesus the Son of God,
let us hold fast our confession.
For we do not have a High Priest
who cannot sympathize with our weaknesses,
but was in all points tempted as we are, yet without sin.
Let us therefore come boldly to the
throne of grace, that we may obtain mercy
and find grace to help in time of need.
—Hebrews 4:14–16

What then shall we say to these things?
If God is for us, who can be against us!
He who did not spare His own Son,
but delivered Him up for us all,
how shall He not with Him also freely give us all things?
Who shall bring a charge against God's elect?
It is God who justifies.
—Romans 8:31–33

Reflection

Truly, when the day of judgement comes,
we shall not be examined as to what we have read,
but what we have done;
not how well we have spoken,
but how we have lived.
—Thomas à Kempis (1380–1471)

Jesus Calls Us O'er the Tumult

Jesus calls us, o'er the tumult
Of our life's wild, restless sea;
Day by day, His sweet voice soundeth
Saying, "Christian, follow me."

As of old, apostles heard it
By the Galilean lake;
Turned from home and toil and kindred,
Leaving all for His dear sake.

Jesus calls us from the worship
Of the vain world's golden store,
From each idol that would keep us,
Saying, "Christian, love Me more."

In our joys and in our sorrows,
Days of toil and hours of ease,
Still He calls, in cares and pleasures,
"Christian, love Me more than these."

Jesus calls us: by Thy mercies
Savior, may we hear Thy call?
Give our hearts to Thy obedience,
Serve and love Thee best of all.

Cecil Francis Alexander (1818–1895)

God's Word

Commit your works to the Lord,
and your thoughts will be established.

...

Everyone proud in heart is an abomination to the Lord;
though they join forces, none will go unpunished.
—Proverbs 16:3, 5

All scripture is given by inspiration of God,
and is profitable for doctrine,
for reproof, for correction,
for instruction in righteousness,
that the man of God may be complete,
thoroughly equipped for every good work.
—2 Timothy 3:16–17

Now this is the confidence that we have in Him,
that if we ask anything according to His will, He hears us.
And if we know that He hears us, whatever we ask,
we know that we have the petitions that we have asked of Him.
—1 John 5:14–15

Reflection

But God is the God of the waves and the billows,
And they are still His when they come over us.
Again and again, we have proved that the
overwhelming thing does not overwhelm.
We were cast down, but not destroyed.
—Amy Carmichael (1867–1951)

Farther Along

Tempted and tried, we're oft made to wonder
Why it should be thus all the day long;
While there are others living about us,
Never molested, though in the wrong.

When death has taken our loved ones,
Leaving our home so lone and so drear;
Then do we wonder why others prosper,
Living so wicked, year after year.

Often, I wonder why I must journey
Over a road so rugged and steep;
While there are others living in comfort,
While with the lost I labor and weep.

"Faithful till death," saith our loving Master,
Short is our time to labor and wait;
Then will our toiling seem to be nothing,
When we shall pass through the heavenly gate.

Soon we will see our dear, loving Savior,
Hear the last trumpet sound through the sky;
Then we will meet those gone on before us,
Then we shall know and understand why.

Farther along we'll know all about it,
Farther along we'll understand why;
Cheer up, my brother, live in the sunshine,
We'll understand it all by and by.

William Buel Stevens (1862–1943)

God's Word

Be sober, be vigilant;
because your adversary the devil
walks about like a roaring lion,
seeking whom he may devour.
Resist him, steadfast in the faith,
knowing that the same sufferings
are experienced by your brotherhood in the world.
But may the God of all grace,
who called us to His eternal glory by Christ Jesus,
after you have suffered a while,
perfect, establish, strengthen, and settle you.
—1 Peter 5:8–11

Blessed be the God and Father of our Lord Jesus Christ,
the Father of mercies and God of all comfort,
who comforts us in all our tribulations.
—2 Corinthians 1:3–4

Reflection

I walked a mile with Pleasure;
She chatted all the way;
But left me none the wiser
For all she had to say.

I walked a mile with Sorrow;
And ne'er a word said she;
But, oh! The things I learned from her,
When Sorrow walked with me.
—Robert Browning Hamilton (ca. 1890)

Grace Greater than Our Sin

Marvelous grace of our loving Lord,
Grace that exceeds our sin and our guilt!
Yonder on Calvary's mount outpoured,
There where the blood of the Lamb was spilled.

Sin and despair, like the sea waves, cold,
Threaten the soul with infinite loss;
Grace that is greater, yes, grace untold,
Points to the refuge, the mighty cross.

Dark is the stain that we cannot hide,
What can avail to wash it away?
Look! There is flowing a crimson tide,
Brighter than snow you may be today.

Marvelous, infinite, matchless grace,
Freely bestowed on all who believe!
You who are longing to see His face,
Will you this moment His grace receive?

Julia Harriette Johnson (1849–1919)

God's Word

For by grace you have been saved through faith,
and that not of yourselves;
it is the gift of God, not of works,
lest anyone should boast.
—Ephesians 2:8–9

My brethren, count it all joy
when you fall into various trials,
knowing that the testing of your faith produces patience.
But let patience have its perfect work,
that you may be perfect and complete, lacking nothing.
—James 1:2–4

For sin shall not have dominion over you,
for you are not under the law but under grace.
—Romans 6:14

Reflection

The law works fear and wrath.
Grace works hope and mercy.
—Martin Luther (1483–1546)

Pass Me Not, O Gentle Savior

Pass me not, O gentle Savior,
Hear my humble cry;
While on others Thou art calling,
Do not pass me by.

Let me at the throne of mercy
Find a sweet relief,
Kneeling there in deep contrition,
Help my unbelief.

Trusting only in Thy merit,
Would I seek Thy face;
Heal my wounded, broken spirit,
Save me by Thy grace.

Thou, the Spring of all my comfort,
More than life to me,
Whom have I on earth beside Thee,
Who in heaven but Thee?

Savior, Savior,
Hear my humble cry;
While on others Thou art calling,
Do not pass me by.

Fanny Jane Crosby (1820–1915)

God's Word

Bow down Your ear, O Lord, hear me;
for I am poor and needy.

. . .

Be merciful to me, O Lord,
for I cry to You all day long.
Rejoice the soul of Your servant,
for to You, O Lord, I lift up my soul.
For you, Lord, are good, and ready to forgive,
and abundant in mercy to all those who call upon You.
Give ear, O Lord, to my prayer;
and attend to the voice of my supplications.
In the day of my trouble I will call upon You,
for You will answer me.
—Psalm 86:1, 3–7

And David said to Gad, "I am in great distress.
Please let us fall into the hand of the Lord,
for His mercies are great;
but do not let me fall into the hand of man."
—2 Samuel 24:14

Reflection

O, My Forgetful Soul,
awake from thy wandering dream;
turn from chasing vanities, look inward, forward, upward,
view thyself,
reflect upon thyself,
dost thou not desire to know God's ways?
—From *The Valley of Vision: A Collection of Puritan Prayers and Devotions*[4]

---

[4] Bennett, *The Valley of Vision: A Collection of Puritan Prayers and Devotions*.

Satisfied

All my life I had a longing
For a drink from some clear spring,
That I hoped would quench the burning
Of the thirst I felt within.

Feeding on the husks around me,
Till my strength was almost gone,
Longed my soul for something better,
Only still to hunger on.

Poor I was, and sought for riches
Something that would satisfy,
But the dust I gathered round me
Only mocked my soul's sad cry.

Well of water, every springing,
Bread of life so rich and free,
Untold wealth that never faileth,
My redeemer is to me.

Hallelujah! I have found Him
Whom my soul so long has craved;
Jesus satisfies my longings,
Through His blood I now am saved.

Clara T. Williams (1858–1937)

God's Word

Then Jesus said to those Jews who believed Him,
"If you abide in My word, you are My disciples indeed.
And you shall know the truth, and the truth shall make you free."
They answered Him "We are Abraham's descendants,
and have never been in bondage to anyone.
How can You say, 'You will be made free'?"
Jesus answered them, "Most assuredly, I say to you,
whoever commits sin is a slave of sin."
—John 8:31–34

Therefore, if anyone is in Christ,
he is a new creation;
old things have passed away;
behold, all things have become new.
—2 Corinthians 5:17

For of Him and through Him
and to Him are all things,
to whom be glory forever.
Amen.
—Romans 11:36

Reflection

Let us leave sadness to the
devil and his angels.
As for us, what can we be but rejoicing and glad?
—Saint Francis of Assisi (1181–1226)

Jesus, Savior, Pilot Me

Jesus, Savior, pilot me
Over life's tempestuous sea;
Unknown waves before me roll,
Hiding rock and treacherous shoal.
Chart and compass come from Thee,
Jesus, Savior, pilot me.

While the Apostles' fragile bark
Struggled with the billows dark,
On the stormy Galilee,
Thou didst walk upon the sea;
And when they beheld Thy form,
Safe they glided through the storm.

Though the sea be smooth and bright,
Sparkling with the stars of night,
And my ship's path be ablaze
With the light of halcyon days,
Still I know my need of Thee;
Jesus, Savior, pilot me.

When the darkling heavens frown,
And the wrathful winds come down,
And the fierce waves, tossed on high,
Lash themselves against the sky,
Jesus, Savior, pilot me,
Over life's tempestuous sea.

When, at last, I near the shore,
And the fearful breakers roar
Twixt me and the peaceful rest,
Then, while leaning on Thy breast,
May I hear Thee say to me,
"Fear not, I will pilot thee."

Edward Hopper (1822–1888)

God's Word

In You, O Lord, I put my trust;
let me never be ashamed;
deliver me in Your righteousness.
Bow down Your ear to me,
deliver me speedily;
be my rock of refuge,
a fortress of defense to save me.
For you are my rock and my fortress;
therefore, for Your name's sake,
lead me and guide me.
—Psalm 31:1–3

Have I not commanded you?
Be strong and of good courage;
do not be afraid, nor be dismayed,
for the Lord your God is with you wherever you go.
—Joshua 1:9

Some trust in chariots, and some in horses;
But we will remember the name of the Lord our God.
—Psalm 20:7

Reflection

Quiet minds that rest in God
cannot be perplexed or frightened,
but go on in fortune or misfortunate
at their private pace,
like a clock during a thunderstorm.
—Robert Louis Stevenson (1850–1894)

Praise to the Lord, The Almighty

Ponder anew
What the Almighty can do;
Who with His love doth befriend thee.

Lord, I'm Coming Home

My soul is sick
My heart is sore;
My strength renew,
My home restore.

I Am Thine, O Lord

I am Thine, O Lord;
I have heard Thy voice
And it spoke Thy love to me;
But I long to rise
In the arms of faith,
And be closer drawn to Thee.

Consecrate me now
To Thy service, Lord,
By the power of grace divine;
Let my soul look up
With a steadfast hope,
And my will be lost in Thine.

O the pure delight
Of a single hour
That before Thy throne I spend;
When I kneel in prayer,
And with Thee, my God,
I commune as friend with friend.

There are depths of love
That I cannot know
Till I cross the narrow sea;
There are heights of joy
That I may not reach
Till I rest in peace with Thee.

Draw me nearer,
Blessed Lord,
To the cross where Thou hast died.
Draw me nearer,
Blessed Lord,
To Thy precious, bleeding side.

Fanny Jane Crosby (1820–1915)

God's Word

Therefore, brethren, having boldness
to enter the Holiest by the blood of Jesus,
by a new and living way which He consecrated for us,
through the veil, that is, His flesh
and having a High Priest over the house of God,
let us draw near with a true heart in full assurance of faith,
having our hearts sprinkled from an evil conscience
and our bodies washed with pure water.
—Hebrews 10:19–22

O Lord, You have searched me and known me.
You know my sitting down and my rising up;
You understand my thought afar off.
You comprehend my path and my lying down,
You are acquainted with all my ways.
—Psalm 139:1–3

Reflection

It is quite natural and inevitable that,
if we spend sixteen hours daily
thinking about the affairs of the world
and five minutes thinking about God,
this world will seem two hundred times more real to us than God.
—William Ralph Inge (1860–1954)

Sun of My Soul

Sun of my soul, Thou Savior dear,
It is not night if Thou be near;
O may no earthborn cloud arise
To hide Thee from Thy servant's eyes.

When the soft dews of kindly sleep
My wearied eyelids gently steep,
Be my last thought, how sweet to rest
Forever on my Savior's breast.

Abide with me from morn till eve,
For without Thee I cannot live;
Abide with me when night is nigh,
For without Thee I dare not die.

If some poor wandering child of Thine
Has spurned today the voice divine,
Now, Lord, the gracious work begin;
Let him no more lie down in sin.

Watch by the sick, enrich the poor
With blessings from Thy boundless store;
Be every mourner's sleep tonight,
Like infants' slumbers, pure and right.

Come near and bless us when we wake,
Ere through the world our way we make,
Till in the ocean of Thy love,
We lose ourselves in Heaven above.

John Kebl (1792–1866)

God's Word

For the Lord God is a sun and shield;
the Lord will give grace and glory;
no good thing will He withhold
from those who walk uprightly.
—Psalm 84:11

Arise, shine;
for your light has come!
And the glory of the Lord is risen upon you.

...

The sun shall no longer be your light by day,
nor the brightness shall the moon give light to you;
but the Lord will be to you an everlasting light,
and your God your glory.
—Isaiah 60:1, 19

To You, O Lord, I lift up my soul.
O my God, I trust in You;
let me not be ashamed;
let not my enemies triumph over me.
—Psalm 25:1–2

Reflection

The greatest glory we can give God
is to distrust our own strength utterly,
and to commit ourselves
wholly to His safe-keeping.
—Brother Lawrence (1614–1691)

Trust and Obey

When we walk with the Lord
In the light of His word,
What a glory He sheds on our way.
When we do His good will,
He abides with us still,
And with all who will trust and obey.

Not a shadow can rise,
Not a cloud in the skies,
But His smile quickly drives it away;
Not a doubt or a fear,
Not a sigh or a tear,
Can abide while we trust and obey.

Not a burden we bear,
Not a sorrow we share,
But our toil He doth richly repay;
Not a grief or a loss,
Not a frown or a cross,
But is blessed if we trust and obey.

But we never can prove
The delight of His love
Until all on the altar we lay;
For the favor He shows,
For the joy He bestows,
Are for them who will trust and obey.

Then in fellowship sweet,
We will sit at His feet,
Or we'll walk by His side in the way;
What He says, we will do,
Where He sends, we will go,
Never fear, only trust and obey.

John H. Sammis (1846–1919)

God's Word

In my distress I called upon the Lord,
and cried out to my God;
He heard my voice from His temple,
and my cry came before Him, even to His ears.
—Psalm 18:6

And we have such trust through Christ toward God.
Not that we are sufficient of ourselves
to think of anything
as being from ourselves,
but our sufficiency is from God.
—2 Corinthians 3:4–5

Every word of God is pure;
He is a shield to those
who put their trust in Him.
—Proverbs 30:5

Reflection

Although it is true that faith brings peace,
it does not always bring it instantaneously.
There may be reasons for the trials of faith,
rather than the rewards of faith.
—Charles Spurgeon (1834–1892)

Praise to the Lord, the Almighty

Praise to the Lord,
The Almighty, the King of creation!
O my soul, praise Him
For He is thy health and salvation!
All ye who hear,
Now to His temple draw near;
Praise Him with glad adoration.

Praise to the Lord,
Who over all things so wondrously reigneth;
Shelters thee under His wings,
Yea, so gently sustaineth.
Hast thou not seen
How thy desires ever have been
Granted in what He ordaineth?

Praise to the Lord,
Who hath fearfully, wondrously, made thee!
Health hath vouchsafed and,
When heedlessly falling, hath stayed thee.
What need or grief
Ever hath failed of relief?
Wings of His mercy did shade thee.

Praise to the Lord,
Who doth prosper thy work and defend thee;
Who from the heavens the streams of
His mercy doth send thee.
Ponder anew
What the Almighty can do;
Who with His love doth befriend thee.

Praise to the Lord,
O let all that is within me adore Him!
All that hath life and breath,
Come now with praises before Him!
Let the "Amen"
Sound from His people again;
Gladly forever we adore Him.

Joachim Neander (1650–1680)
Translated from German to English by Catherine Winkworth (1827–1878)

God's Word

Make a joyful shout to God, all the earth!
Sing out the honor of His name;
make His praise glorious.
Say to God,
"How awesome are Your works!
Through the greatness of Your power
Your enemies shall submit themselves to You.
All the earth shall worship You and sing praises to You;
They shall sing praises to Your name."
—Psalm 66:1–4

Oh, give thanks to the Lord!
Call upon His name;
make known His deeds among the peoples!
Sing to Him, sing psalms to Him;
talk of all His wondrous works!
—1 Chronicles 16:8–9

Reflection

The Doxology

Praise God from whom all blessings flow;
Praise Him all creatures here below;
Praise Him above, ye heavenly host:
Praise Father, Son and Holy Ghost.
Amen.
—Anglican bishop Thomas Ken (1637–1711)

He Hideth My Soul

A wonderful Savior is Jesus, my Lord,
A wonderful Savior to me.
He hideth my soul in the cleft of the rock,
Where rivers of pleasure I see.

A wonderful Savior is Jesus, my Lord,
He taketh my burdens away;
He holdeth me up, and I shall not be moved,
He giveth me strength as my day.

With numberless blessings each moment He crowns,
And filled with His fullness divine,
I sing in my rapture, "O, glory to God,"
For such a Redeemer as mine.

When clothed in His brightness, transported I rise
To meet Him in clouds of the sky,
His perfect salvation, His wonderful love,
I'll shout with the millions on high.

He hideth my soul in the cleft of the rock
That covers the dry, thirsty land.
He hideth my life with the depths of His love,
And covers me there with His hand.

Fanny Jane Crosby (1820–1915)

God's Word

For in the time of trouble
He shall hide me in His pavilion;
in the secret place of His tabernacle
He shall hide me;
He shall set me high upon a rock.
—Psalm 27:5

And the Lord said, "Here is a place by Me,
and you shall stand on the rock.
So it shall be, while My glory passes by,
that I will put you in the cleft of the rock,
and will cover you with My hand while I pass by."
—Exodus 33:21–22

Keep me as the apple of Your eye;
hide me under the shadow of Your wings,
from the wicked who oppress me,
from my deadly enemies who surround me.
—Psalm 17:8–9

Reflection

If the blind put their hand in God's,
they find their way more surely
than those who see but have not faith or purpose.
—Helen Keller (1880–1968)

Blest Be the Tie That Binds

Blest be the tie that binds
Our hearts in Christian love;
The fellowship of kindred minds
Is like to that above.

Before our Father's throne
We pour our ardent prayers;
Our fears, our hopes, our aims are one
Our comforts and our cares.

We share each other's woes,
Our mutual burdens bear;
And often for each other flows
The sympathizing tear.

When we asunder part,
It gives us inward pain;
But we shall still be joined in heart,
And hope to meet again.

This glorious hope revives
Our courage by the way;
While each in expectation lives
And longs to see the day.

From sorrow, toil and pain,
And sin, we shall be free,
And perfect love and friendship reign
Through all eternity.

John Fawcett (1739–1817)

God's Word

But if we walk in the light
as He is in the light,
we have fellowship with one another,
and the blood of Jesus Christ His Son,
cleanses us from all sin.
—1 John 1:7

Let love be without hypocrisy.
Abhor what is evil.
Cling to what is good.
Be kindly affectionate to one another
with brotherly love,
in honor giving preference to one another.
—Romans 12:9–10

And above all things
have fervent love for one another,
for "love will cover a multitude of sins."
—1 Peter 4:8

Reflection

Without distinction,
Without calculation,
Without procrastination,
Love.
—Henry Drummond (1851–1897)

Beneath the Cross of Jesus

Beneath the cross of Jesus I fain would take my stand;
The shadow of a mighty rock within a weary land,
A home within the wilderness, a rest upon the way,
From the burning of the noontide heat and the burden of the day.

O safe and happy shelter, O refuge, tried and sweet,
O trysting place where heaven's love and heaven's justice meet.
As to the holy patriarch that wondrous dream was given,
So seems my Savior's cross to me, a ladder up to heaven.

There lies beneath its shadow, but on the further side,
The darkness of an awful grave that gapes both deep and wide.
And there between us stands the cross, two arms outstretched to save,
A watchman set to guard the way from that eternal grave.

Upon that cross of Jesus, mine eyes at times can see
The very dying form of One who suffered there for me;
And from my stricken heart with tears, two wonders I confess;
The wonders of redeeming love and my unworthiness.

I take, O cross, thy shadow for my abiding place;
I ask no other sunshine than the sunshine of His face;
Content to let the world go by, to know no gain or loss;
My sinful self my only shame, my glory all the cross.

Elizabeth Cecelia Douglas Clephane (1830–1869)

God's Word

But what things were gain to me,
these I have counted loss for Christ.
Yet indeed I also count all things loss for the excellence
of the knowledge of Christ Jesus my Lord,
for whom I have suffered the loss of all things,
and count them as rubbish, that I may gain Christ.
—Philippians 3:7–8

But you are a chosen generation,
a royal priesthood, a holy nation,
His own special people,
that you may proclaim the praises of Him
who called you out of darkness into His marvelous light.
—1 Peter 2:9

For I am not ashamed of the gospel of Christ,
for it is the power of God
to salvation for everyone who believes.
—Romans 1:16

Reflection

The lawyer can deliver his client but from strife,
The physician can deliver his patient but from sickness,
The master can deliver his servant but from bondage,
But the Lord delivereth us from all.
—Henry Smith (1560–1591)

Lord, I'm Coming Home

I've wondered far away from God,
The paths of sin too long I've trod,
Lord, I'm coming home.

I've wasted many precious years,
I now repent with bitter tears,
Lord, I'm coming home.

I'm tired of sin and straying, Lord,
I'll trust Thy love, believe Thy word,
Lord, I'm coming home.

My soul is sick, my heart is sore,
My strength renew, my home restore,
Lord, I'm coming home.

My only hope, my only plea,
That Jesus died, and died for me,
Lord, I'm coming home.

I need His cleansing blood I know,
Oh, wash me whiter than the snow.
Lord, I'm coming home.

Coming home, coming home,
Nevermore to roam;
Open now Thine arms of love,
Lord, I'm coming home.

Williams J. Kirkpatrick (1838–1921)

God's Word

If we say that we have no sin, we deceive ourselves,
and the truth is not in us.
If we confess our sins, He is faithful and just
to forgive us our sins and to cleanse us from all unrighteousness.
—1 John 1:8–9

But when he came to himself, he said,
"How many of my father's hired servants have
bread enough and to spare, and I perish with hunger!
I will arise and go to my father, and will say to him,
'Father, I have sinned against heaven and before you,
and I am no longer worthy to be called your son.
Make me like one of your hired servants.'"
—Luke 15:17–19

What then shall I do with Jesus who is called Christ?
—Matthew 27:22

Reflection

I have studied many religions,
many different persuasions of thought in Christian belief,
and I have come to this:
the most important question in anyone's life
is the question asked by poor Pilate in Matthew 27:22:
"What shall I do, then, with Jesus who is called Christ?"
No other question in the whole sweep
of human experience is as important as this.
It is the choice between life and death,
between meaningless existence and life abundant.
—Dale Evans (1912–2001)

A Mighty Fortress Is Our God

A mighty fortress is our God,
A bulwark never failing;
Our helper, He, amid the flood of mortal ills prevailing.
For still our ancient foe doth seek to work us woe;
His craft and power are great, and armed with cruel hate;
On earth is not his equal.

Did we in our own strength confide,
Our striving would be losing;
Were not the right Man on our side, the Man of God's own choosing.
Dost ask who that may be? Christ Jesus, it is He;
Lord Sabaoth, His Name, from age to age the same,
And He must win the battle.

And though this world, with devils filled,
Should threaten to undo us,
We will not fear, for God hath willed
His truth to triumph through us.
The prince of darkness grim, we tremble not for him;
His rage we can endure, for lo, his doom is sure,
One little word shall fell him.

That world above all earthly powers,
No thanks to them abideth;
The Spirit and the gifts are ours through Him who with us sideth.
Let goods and kindred go, this mortal life also;
The body they may kill: God's truth abideth still;
His kingdom is forever!

Martin Luther (1483–1546)
Translated from German to English by
Frederick H. Hedge (1805–1890)

God's Word

O God, do not be far from me;
O my God make haste to help me!
Let them be confounded and consumed
who are adversaries of my life;
let them be covered with reproach and dishonor
who seek my hurt.
But I will hope continually,
and will praise You yet more and more.
My mouth shall tell of Your righteousness
and Your salvation all the day,
for I do not know their limits.
I will go in the strength of the Lord God;
I will make mention of Your righteousness,
of Yours only.
—Psalm 71:12–16

The name of the Lord is a strong tower;
the righteous run to it and are safe.
—Proverbs 18:10

Reflection

Faith is the refusal to panic—
No matter the circumstances.
—Martyn Lloyd-Jones (1899–1981)

O Love That Will Not Let Me Go

O love that will not let me go,
I rest my weary soul in Thee;
I give Thee back the life I owe,
That in Thine ocean depths
Its flow may richer, fuller be.

O light that follows all my way,
I yield my flickering torch to Thee;
My heart restores its borrowed ray,
That in Thy sunshine's blaze
Its day may brighter, fairer be.

O joy that seekest me through pain,
I cannot close my heart to Thee;
I trace the rainbow through the rain,
And feel the promise is not vain,
That morn shall tearless be.

O cross that liftest up my head,
I dare not ask to fly from Thee;
I lay in dust life's glory dead,
And from the ground there blossoms red,
Life that shall endless be.

George Matheson (1842–1906)

God's Word

Therefore know that the Lord your God, He is God,
the faithful God who keeps covenant and mercy
for a thousand generations
with those who love Him and keep His commandments.
—Deuteronomy 7:9

The Lord has appeared of old to me, saying:
"Yes, I have loved you with an everlasting love;
therefore with lovingkindness I have drawn you."
—Jeremiah 31:3

For I, the Lord your God,
will hold your right hand,
saying to you, "Fear not, I will help you."
—Isaiah 41:13

Reflection

Born in Glasgow, Scotland, Matheson's wedding engagement
was broken when his fiancée learned he would soon become
blind. In great sorrow, he penned the immortal words of "O
Love That Will Not Let Me Go." He never married.

There's a Wideness in God's Mercy

But we make His love too narrow
By false limits of our own,
And we magnify His strictness
With a zeal He will not own.

Sweet Hour of Prayer

In seasons of distress and grief,
My soul has often found relief,
And often escaped the tempter's snare
By thy return, sweet hour of prayer.

There's a Wideness in God's Mercy

There's a wideness in God's mercy like the wideness of the sea;
There's a kindness in God's justice which is more than liberty.

There is no place where earth's sorrows are
more felt than up in heaven;
There is no place where earth's failings have
such kindly judgment given.

There is welcome for the sinner and more graces for the good;
There is mercy with the Savior, there is healing in His blood.

For the love of God is broader than the measure of the mind,
And the heart of the Eternal is most wonderfully kind.

There is plentiful redemption in the blood that has been shed;
There is joy for all the members in the sorrow of the Head.

If our love were but more simple, we should take Him at His word.
And our lives would be thanksgiving for the goodness of our Lord.

Trouble souls, why will you scatter like a crowd of frightened sheep?
Foolish hearts, why will you wander from a love so true and deep?

But we make His love too narrow by false limits of our own;
And we magnify His strictness with a zeal He will not own.

Was there ever kinder Shepherd, half so gentle, half so sweet,
As the Savior who would have us come and gather at His feet?

Frederick W. Faber (1814–1863)

God's Word

Now the Lord descended in the cloud
and stood with him there,
and proclaimed the name of the Lord.
And the Lord passed before him and proclaimed,
"The Lord, the Lord God, merciful and gracious,
longsuffering, and abounding in goodness and truth.
Keeping mercy for thousands,
forgiving iniquity and transgression and sin."
—Exodus 34:5–7

Can you search out the deep things of God?
Can you find out the limits of the Almighty?
They are higher than heaven—what can you do?
Deeper than Sheol—what can you know?
Their measure is longer than the earth
and broader than the sea.
—Job 11:7–9

Reflection

The greatest single distinguishing feature
of the omnipotence of God
is that our imagination gets lost just thinking about it.
—Blaise Pascal (1623–1662)

Sweet Hour of Prayer

Sweet hour of prayer!
That calls me from a world of care,
And bids me at my Father's throne,
Make all my wants and wishes known.
In seasons of distress and grief,
My soul has often found relief,
And oft' escaped the tempter's snare,
By thy return, sweet hour of prayer.

Sweet hour of prayer!
The joys I feel, the bliss I share,
Of those whose anxious spirits burn
With strong desires for thy return.
With such I hasten to the place
Where God, my Savior, shows His face,
And gladly take my station there
And wait for thee, sweet hour of prayer.

Sweet hour of prayer!
Thy wings shall my petition bear
To Him whose truth and faithfulness
Engage the waiting soul to bless.
And since He bids me seek His face,
Believe His Word and trust His grace,
I'll cast on Him my every care,
And wait for thee, sweet hour of prayer.

Sweet hour of prayer!
May I thy consolation share,
Till from Mount Pisgah's lofty height,
I view my home and take my flight,
This robe of flesh I'll drop and rise
To seize the everlasting prize,
And shout, while passing through the air,
"Farewell, farewell, sweet hour of prayer!"

William W. Walford (1772–1850)

God's Word

Then the Lord appeared to Solomon by night,
and said to him:
"I have heard your prayer, and have chosen
this place for Myself as a house of sacrifice.

. . .

"If My people who are called by My name
will humble themselves,
and pray and seek My face,
and turn from their wicked ways,
then I will hear from heaven,
and will forgive their sin and heal their land."
—2 Chronicles 7:12, 14

Is anyone among you suffering?
Let him pray.
—James 5:13

"And when you pray,
do not use vain repetitions as the heathen do.
For they think that they will be heard
for their many words."
—Matthew 6:7

Reflection

As a sound may dislodge an avalanche,
so the prayer of faith sets in motion the power of God.
—Lettie Burd Cowman (1870–1960)

Spirit of God, Descend upon My Heart

Spirit of God, descend upon my heart;
Wean it from sin, through all its pulses move.
Stoop to my weakness, mighty as Thou art,
And make me love You as I ought to love.

I ask no dream, no prophet ecstasies,
No sudden reading of the veil of clay,
No angel visitant, no opening skies;
But take the dimness of my soul away.

Teach me to feel that You are always nigh;
Teach me the struggles of the soul to bear,
To check the rising doubt, the rebel sigh;
Teach me the patience of unanswered prayer.

Did you not bid us love You, God and King;
Love you with all our heart and strength and mind?
I see Thy cross; there teach my heart to cling;
O let me see You, and O, let me find.

Teach me to love You as Your angels love,
One holy passion filling all my frame;
The fullness of the heaven-descended Dove,
My heart an altar, and Your love the flame.

George Croly (1780–1860)

God's Word

You shall love the Lord your God
with all your heart, with all your soul,
and with all your strength.
And these words which I command you today shall be in your heart.
You shall teach them diligently to your children,
and shall talk of them when you sit in your house,
when you walk by the way,
when you lie down,
and when you rise up.

. . .

You shall write them on the doorposts of your house
and on your gates.
—Deuteronomy 6:5–7, 9

Only fear the Lord,
and serve Him in truth with all your heart;
for consider what great things He has done for you.
—1 Samuel 12:24

A good man obtains favor from the Lord,
but a man of wicked intentions He will condemn.
—Proverbs 12:2

Reflection

Between God and the Soul,
there is no between.
—Julian of Norwich (1342–1416)

The Old Account Settled

There was a time on earth, when in the book of heaven
An old account was standing for sins yet unforgiven;
My name was at the top, with many things below—
I went unto the Keeper and settled long ago.

The old account was large and growing every day,
For I was always sinning and never tried to pay,
But when I looked ahead and saw such pain and woe,
I said that I would settle, I settled long ago.

When at the Judgement Bar, I stand before the King,
And He the book will open and cannot find a thing,
Then will my heart be glad while tears of joy will flow
Because I had it settled, I settled long ago.

When in that happy home, my Savior's home above,
I'll sing redemption's story, and praise Him for His love;
I'll not forget that book, with pages white as snow,
Because I came and settled, I settled long ago.

O sinner, seek the Lord, repent of all your sins,
For thus He hath commanded, if you would enter in;
And then if you should live a hundred years below,
Up there, you'll not regret it, you settled long ago.

Frank M. Graham (1859–1931)

God's Word

Look to Me, and be saved,
all you ends of the earth!
For I am God and there is no other.
I have sworn by Myself;
the word has gone out of My mouth in righteousness,
and shall not return,
that to Me every knee shall bow,
every tongue shall take an oath.
—Isaiah 45:22–23

But why do you judge your brother?
Or why do you show contempt for your brother?
For we shall all stand before the judgement seat of Christ.
For it is written:
"As I live, says the Lord,
every knee shall bow to Me,
and every tongue shall confess to God."
So then each of us shall give account of himself to God.
—Romans 14:10–12

Reflection

If you believe what you like in the Gospels,
and reject what you do not like,
it is not the Gospels you believe in,
but yourself.
—Saint Augustine (354-430)

Now Thank We All Our God

Now thank we all our God,
With heart and hands and voices,
Who wondrous things has done,
In Whom this world rejoices;
Who from our mother's arms
Has blessed us on our way,
With countless gifts of love,
And still is ours today.

O may this bounteous God,
Through all our life be near us,
With ever joyful hearts
And blessed peace to cheer us;
And keep us in His grace,
And guide us when perplexed,
And free us from all ills,
In this world and the next

All praise and thanks to God
The Father now be given;
The Son and Him Who reigns
With Them in highest heaven;
The one eternal God,
Whom earth and heaven adore;
For this it was, is now,
And shall be ever more.

Martin Rinkart (1586–1649)
Translated from German to English by Catherine Winkworth (1827–1878)

God's Word

Then out of them shall proceed thanksgiving
and the voice of those who make merry;
I will multiply them, and they shall not diminish;
I will also glorify them, and they shall not be small.
—Jeremiah 30:19

Enter into His gates with thanksgiving,
and into His courts with praise.
Be thankful to Him, and bless His name.
For the Lord is good;
His mercy is everlasting,
and His truth endures to all generations.
—Psalm 100:4–5

Thanks be to God for His indescribable gift!
—2 Corinthians 9:15

Reflection

Keep your eyes open to your many mercies.
The man who forgets to be thankful
has fallen asleep in life.
—Robert Louis Stevenson (1850–1894)

He Rolled the Sea Away

When Israel out of bondage came,
A sea before them lay;
My Lord reached down His mighty hand
And rolled the sea away.

Before me was a sea of sin
So great, I feared to pray;
My heart's desire the Savior read,
And rolled the sea away.

When sorrows dark, like stormy waves,
Were dashing over my way,
Again the Lord in mercy came,
And rolled the sea away.

And when I reach the sea of death,
For needed grace I'll pray;
I know my Lord will quickly come,
And roll the sea away.

Then, forward still—'tis Jehovah's will!
Though the billows dash and spray,
With a conquering tread, we will push ahead;
He'll roll the sea away!

Henry J. Zelley (1859–1942)

God's Word

Then the word of the Lord came to Jeremiah, saying,
"Behold, I am the Lord, the God of all flesh.
Is there anything too hard for Me?"
—Jeremiah 32:26–27

You shall fear the Lord your God;
You shall serve Him,
and to Him you shall hold fast,
and take oaths in His name.
He is your praise, and He is your God,
who has done for you these great
and awesome things which your eyes have seen.
—Deuteronomy 10:20–21

Oh, magnify the Lord with me,
and let us exalt His name together.
I sought the Lord, and He heard me,
and delivered me from all my fears.
—Psalm 34:3–4

Reflection

Catch on fire with enthusiasm for God
and people will come from miles around
to watch you burn.
—John Wesley (1703–1791)

How Firm a Foundation

How firm a foundation,
Ye saints of the Lord,
Is laid for your faith in His excellent Word.
What more can He say than to you He hath said,
To you who for refuge to Jesus have fled?

"Fear not, I am with thee, oh, be not dismayed,
For I am thy God, and will still give thee aid;
I'll strengthen thee, help thee, and cause thee to stand,
Upheld by My gracious, omnipotent hand.

"When through the deep waters
I call thee to go,
The rivers of sorrow shall not overflow;
For I will be with thee thy trouble to bless,
And sanctify to thee they deepest distress.

"When through fiery trials
Thy pathway shall lie,
My grace, all sufficient, shall be thy supply;
The flame shall not hurt thee—I only design
Thy dross to consume and thy gold to refine.

"The soul that on Jesus
Hath leaned for repose,
I will not, I will not desert to his foes;
That soul, though all hell should endeavor to shake,
I will never, no never, no never forsake!"

First appeared in John Rippon's *Selection of Hymns*, 1787.
These famous words are attributed only to "K."

God's Word

· Listen to me, O Jacob
And Israel, My called;
I am He, I am the First,
I am also the Last.
Indeed My hand has laid the foundation of the earth,
And My right hand has stretched out the heavens;
When I call to them
They stand up together.
—Isaiah 48:12–13

He only is my rock and my salvation;
He is my defense;
I shall not be greatly moved.
—Psalm 62:2

In the beginning was the Word,
and the Word was with God,
and the Word was God.
He was in the beginning with God.
All things were made through Him,
. and without Him nothing was made that was made.
—John 1:1–3

Reflection

It is impossible to rightly govern the world
without God and the Bible.
—George Washington (1732–1799)

It Is Well with My Soul

When peace, like a river, attendeth my way,
When sorrows like sea billows roll;
Whatever my lot, Thou hast taught me to say,
It is well, it is well, with my soul.

Tho' Satan should buffet, though trials should come,
Let this blest assurance control,
That Christ hath regarded my helpless estate,
And hath shed His own blood for my soul.

My sin—oh, the bliss of this glorious thought!—
My sin, not in part, but the whole,
Is nailed to the cross and I bear it no more,
Praise the Lord, Praise the Lord, O my soul!

But, Lord, 'tis for Thee, for Thy coming we wait,
The sky, not the grave is our goal;
Oh, trump of the angel! Oh, voice of the Lord!
Blessed hope, blessed rest of my soul.

And, Lord, haste the day when the faith shall be sight,
The clouds be rolled back as a scroll;
The trump shall resound, and the Lord shall descend,
Even so, it is well with my soul.

Horatio G. Spafford (1828–1888)

God's Word

My soul, wait silently for God alone,
for my expectation is from Him.

...

In God is my salvation and my glory;
the rock of my strength,
and my refuge, is in God.
Trust in Him at all times, you people;
pour out your heart before Him;
God is a refuge for us.
—Psalm 62:5, 7–8

Though He slay me,
yet will I trust Him.
—Job 13:15

Blessed is the man who trusts
in the Lord, and whose hope
is in the Lord.
—Jeremiah 17:7

Reflection

In Gethsemane, the holiest of all petitioners
prayed three times that a certain cup might pass from Him.
It did not.
—C. S. Lewis (1898–1963)

Now the Day Is Over

Now the day is over,
Night is drawing nigh,
Shadows of the evening
Steal across the sky.

Now the darkness gathers,
Stars begin to peep,
Bird, and beasts and flowers
Soon will be asleep.

Jesus, give the weary
Calm and sweet repose;
With Thy tenderest blessing
May mine eyelids close.

Grant to little children
Visions bright of Thee;
Guard the sailors tossing
On the deep, blue sea.

Comfort those who suffer,
Watching late in pain;
Those who plan some evil
From their sin restrain.

Through the long night watches
May Thine angels spread
Their white wings above me,
Watching round my bed.

When the morning wakens,
Then may I arise
Pure and fresh and sinless
In Thy holy eyes.

Glory to the Father,
Glory to the Son,
And to Thee, blest Spirit,
While all ages run.

Sabine Baring-Gould (1834–1924)

God's Word

But You, O Lord, are a shield for me,
my glory and the One who lifts up my head.
I cried to the Lord with my voice,
and He heard me from His holy hill.
I lay down and slept;
I awoke, for the Lord sustained me.
I will not be afraid of ten thousands of people
who have set themselves against me all around.
—Psalm 3:3–6

For thus says the Lord God, the Holy One of Israel:
"In returning and rest you shall be saved;
in quietness and confidence shall be your strength."
—Isaiah 30:15

Every good gift and every perfect gift is from above,
and comes down from the Father of lights,
with whom there is no variation or shadow of turning.
—James 1:17

Reflection

When you rise in the morning,
give thanks for the light, for your life,
for your strength.
Give thanks for your food and for the joy of living.
If you see no reason to give thanks,
the fault lies in yourself.
—Chief Tecumseh (1768–1813)

God Be with You till We Meet Again

God be with you till we meet again;
By His counsels guide, uphold you,
With His sheep securely fold you,
God be with you till we meet again.

God be with you till we meet again;
'Neath His wings, protecting, hide you.
Daily manna still provide you;
God be with you till we meet again.

God be with you till we meet again;
When life's perils thick confound you,
Put His arms unfailing 'round you.
God be with you till we meet again.

God be with you till we meet again;
Keep love's banner floating over you.
Smite death's threatening wave before you,
God be will you till we meet again.

Jeremiah Eames Ranker (1828–1904)

God's Word

Again I say to you that if two of you agree
on earth concerning anything that they ask,
it will be done for them by My Father in heaven.
For where two or three are gathered together in My name,
I am there in the midst of them.
—Matthew 18:19–20

A new commandment I give to you,
that you love one another; as I have loved you,
that you also love one another.
By this all will know that you are My disciples,
if you have love for one another.
—John 13:34–35

Rejoice with those who rejoice,
and weep with those who weep.
Be of the same mind toward one another.
—Romans 12:15–16

Reflection

Thee lift me, and I lift thee,
And together we ascend.
—John Greenleaf Whittier (1807–1892)

About the Author

Patty Ellis is a former model, concert pianist, recording artist, and motivational speaker who achieved national acclaim with her inspirational guide for teenagers, Girl Power. As a frequent guest on countless national television talk shows and local television and radio programs, Patty shared a dynamic message of encouragement and  advice that resonated with thousands of young women throughout the United States and Japan. Ellis currently resides in Houston, Texas.